Better Government
THROUGH **Better Hiring**

To Bobbie,

It took long enough
but the book is finally
in print. Thanks for
All you hard work.

Best,

Ken

Better Government
THROUGH Better Hiring

A Must-Read for Americans

K. B. Slutzky

***BOOK*LOGIX˙**
Alpharetta, GA

ISBN: 978-1-6653-0282-1 - Paperback
eISBN: 978-1-6653-0283-8 - eBook

Library of Congress Control Number: 2021915998

Printed in the United States of America   0 8 1 7 2 1

♾ This paper meets the requirements of ANSI/NISO Z39.48-1992 (Permanence of Paper)

Writing this book was a major undertaking.
As I generally do when I tackle a big job, I used a
team approach. I want to dedicate this book to those who
contributed. In no particular order, they are David, Denise, Ben,
Gabriele, Dan, Bobbie, Meghan, Annette, Heather, Jerry, Susan,
Dick, Matthew, Naren, Hope, Hobbs, Justin, Clay, and Julia.
Without them, I would not and could not have
completed this project. Thank you!

"It is not necessary to change. Survival is not mandatory." [1]

–W. Edwards Deming

Contents

Introduction

"The world as we have created it is a process of our thinking. It cannot be changed without changing our thinking." [1]

–Albert Einstein

For the last twenty years, I have been frustrated by and disgusted with our election system and the choices I faced during each general election. I never saw ballots with the names of those I thought best suited for high office. And those who did get elected were stymied by our governmental systems and culture. Each time the party in the White House changed, the new administration began to undo what the previous administration had done. Each party did virtually anything to prevent the other from doing something, especially if it was good for the country. At election time, which seemed to be constant, I witnessed nothing but character assassination and deplorable conduct. The assault on the Capitol sealed the deal. I had to try to bring about some change.

America was and should have been shaken to its core by the events leading up to and immediately following the election of 2020. We handled the immediate crisis, but new and possibly much worse events are likely just beyond the horizon. We have deep and complicated issues to address. This book provides enough detail to show that the problems are real, the problems need to be analyzed carefully, and a path forward must be determined.

"Anyone willing to do what is required to become president of the United States is thereby barred from taking that office." [2]

–Alan Greenspan

Alan Greenspan is a bright individual, and as chairman of the Federal Reserve, he worked for several presidents. He has first-hand knowledge of their character because he was in office while they were running for president and served under them after they became president. His comment, while somewhat humorous, is profound. He is saying that our election system only permits attainment of the presidency by those whose personality is unsuitable for a president. The corollary is that those who are suitable to hold the office of president will not get elected under the current system.

We need to make changes to our systems of governance if we are to have any hope of getting out of our current predicament. Our election system is a good starting place for two reasons. First, it is obviously flawed when it repeatedly produces results that are unsatisfactory, results that reflect a system that does the opposite of what it is supposed to do. Second, it is somewhat easier to change than other aspects of governance because the election system is based on traditions and not the Constitution. This book examines the current election system, discusses the elements of a better system, and explores how to move to a "hiring" system that could produce better results.

> "It is time for us to do what we were hired
> to do by the American people."
>
> **–Kamala Harris**

Vice President Kamala Harris made this remark on national television right before her inauguration. It was insightful in two respects. First, the processes for hiring someone and electing someone have a great deal in common. Second, she was "hired" by the American people through a process that Americans own and that Americans can change.

I am not a politician. I am an engineer by education and a problem solver by nature. I received my degree from West Point in 1965 and spent five years in the Army. One of those years was in Vietnam. A great deal of my knowledge about problem solving comes from working for Procter & Gamble (P&G), which is a world-class organization. I also have extensive experience hiring people. I spent over fifteen years as the head of operations and personnel for a national company.

The most important lesson I learned about problem solving is that we are unlikely to solve a problem if we don't know we have one. In hiring, I learned that there are great tools and techniques to help make better decisions. This knowledge applies to electing public servants, too.

This book examines our systems of governance and especially our election system, which is in essence a hiring system. The material also has broader applications. Because most people look for a job at least once in their lives, and many will engage in hiring others, knowledge about hiring can be beneficial to everyone. Life is a series of "problems," whether positive or negative. Problem-solving skills can aid in getting anything done, so time spent learning how to solve problems is also time well spent.

I have included some humor because we can never laugh enough. You will find that each chapter starts and ends with quotes. These quotes, with few exceptions, are relevant to the subject matter. All were made by widely respected individuals. The exceptions are there because they are funny. If you learn anything from this book and snicker at least once, I've met two of my goals. If you think hard about our problems, I'll be happy. If you decide it's time to do something to bring about much-needed change, I'll be ecstatic. I'll give you an idea along those lines at the very end of the book.

It is time Americans realized we can't use the same election system repeatedly and expect a better result. The current system might produce different names but not a different outcome. This is a problem we must recognize and address. A system produces what it is designed to produce and nothing significantly different until it is replaced by a system that is constructed differently. We can take heart in that the system now in use is a problem-solver's dream. We could make it better in many ways.

It is also time to embrace change in many other areas of governance. The evidence is all around us, but we shield our eyes and make believe everything is fine. We need to open our eyes and our minds and make better choices about the people we elect and the way they conduct our business.

Chapter 1

Problem Recognition

"The big problems are where people don't realize they have one in the first place." [1]

–W. Edwards Deming

I n 1968 and 1969, I was in the Army in Vietnam. I was the commander of a company that maintained a highway critical to
the flow of goods and personnel between two cities. One of those
cities was Dak To, the jumping-off point for many major offen-
sives that North Vietnam launched. The Tet Offensive came
through Dak To in January 1968. After completing my command
time, I became an intelligence officer for the northern half of
Vietnam for an engineer brigade. An intelligence officer collected
enemy-attack reports from brigade units and other headquarters.
He then tried to make sense out of them as to the tactics employed,
the strength of the enemy, and the timing of future attacks. He
disseminated the information to the brigade units to help them
deal with the ever-changing threats. As a company commander, I

received these reports and found them boring and uninformative. A typical report might start like this: "During the last week, there were ten sapper attacks throughout the brigade that produced two KIA (killed in action) and the destruction of . . ."

If reports were boring, were the right people even reading them? I saw the problem and took a different approach. Reports I prepared might have started this way: "On the night of January 22, there was no moon and the cloud cover was heavy. Chi and Duc had been waiting for just such a night. They tied satchels of explosives around their waists and slipped into the stream that went under the fence surrounding the road-maintenance-equipment yard. Once under the barbed wire and on dry ground, Duc knew where to go because he visited the installation weekly as a barber. He liked the soldiers; at least he acted that way. Under the cover of dark, he made his way to a bulldozer and attached a block of C-4 explosives to . . ."

My reports got read. Perhaps they even saved lives.

This story does two things. It exemplifies a concept central to this book: continuous improvement. We must never stop looking for ways to do things better. It also illustrates the value of story-telling rather than lecturing. For this reason, I often use stories to illustrate my points. I have written books, lesson plans, sales brochures, magazine articles, and letters. Stories get my points across and make for enjoyable reading. I hope you find the stories enjoyable and enlightening.

Every story is based on real events. I might have changed the specifics for a variety of reasons, including that most happened more than fifty years ago and that I rarely remember what I had for lunch. Some stories make me look good. Some will not. A few will be embarrassing. The goal remains the same: inform, stimulate open-minded thinking, and keep you from falling asleep.

This chapter introduces the concept of continuous improvement, a concept of great importance. As the quote under the chapter title hints, this chapter is about the first step in solving a problem: coming to the realization that there is a problem. The use of quotes at the start of each chapter is intended to set the stage for the material in that chapter.

At age ten, I was a little thief in two respects: I stole small amounts of money and I used little fingers to succeed. I am not proud of my behavior and won't brag that I was good at it and never caught. This story and many others throughout the book make important points, however.

I was motivated to steal because I wanted a bigger engine for one of the model airplanes I'd built. *Wants* can also be classified as *needs*. I had completed the construction, but I didn't have the money to buy the engine. It would take me months to save the money, so I became a thief. I had other options, but I chose thievery because it was tempting and looked easy.

My father owned a tavern. He brought home an advertising gimmick, a huge liquor bottle about two feet high with a base that measured about eighteen inches on all four sides. It had a narrow neck like a typical bottle. He put the thing on the floor of the linen closet and closed the door. For quite some time, he dropped his loose quarters into the bottle. When my "wants" got the best of me, the bottle held several inches of quarters. I observed that the falling quarters had broken out a back corner of the bottle just big enough for me to stick my skinny fingers through and take out a few quarters at a time. Those quarters called to me.

I was a smart thief. I never took quarters when anyone was home. But I was home alone a lot. My mother had died the year before. My father worked from four in the afternoon to four in the morning. I had two older brothers, but we had different school hours. We had a live-in housekeeper, but she went out shopping regularly. I could get into the closet, be careful not to cut my fingers, grab one or two quarters at a time so the loss would not be detected, and be finished in two minutes. In a few months, I had enough money to meet my "needs," so I stopped. My thievery went unnoticed.

The theft of money was a problem, but nobody realized it. Without knowing there is a problem, the only way it can go away is by accident or a change in circumstances. My father could have discovered the break in the bottle, decided it wasn't a good bank, taken the money out, and thrown the bottle in the trash. He could have decided he would be better off taking the quarters to the bank, depositing them, and earning interest. As it happened, I reached my goal and stopped stealing, leaving the issue unresolved. But it was no longer a problem. It would have been better for my self-esteem if I had developed a guilty conscience and returned the money, but I didn't. The lesson is that you can't solve a problem if you don't know the problem exists or don't perceive it as a problem.

My admission to thievery has a lesson that applies to problem solving. We will start by analyzing the first step, recognizing there is a problem, and then build a problem-solving methodology.

Try to imagine the difficulty of realizing that our election system is problematic and that the problems will not go away as a result of an accident or a change in circumstances. How do you get a nation of people to reach the conclusion that our system has a problem? How can we make people see that the whole system is terribly flawed? How can we find an acceptable way to address the problem?

You have to start at the end of the system. Look at the results you are getting and compare those with what your objectives were and what results other election systems are producing. No one individual or country has a lock on the best way to get something done. There is a management concept that is referred to as Best Practices. Using Best Practices, you don't need to reinvent the wheel to solve a problem. You look to others who have dealt with the same type of problem and borrow from them. Doing so gives you a tremendous advantage. You can examine the system you borrowed and look for flaws that have come up. In your new system, you take the best of that other system and delete anything that wasn't working. First, however, we must come to the realization that we have a problem.

Consider the last few presidential elections. With the vote counting that took place in Florida, the George Bush election ended bitterly. Throughout the Obama election, and even after, the public argued repeatedly about whether he could even be president because they could not agree on where he was born. Then we had the Trump/Clinton fiasco. Sadly, if one of our primary goals was to divide the country, we could not have had a better system or outcome, an outcome that happens to be insignificant compared to the Trump/Biden election.

When our election process leads to negativity, division, and riots, we have a problem. We have to define that problem and address it with the best people and the best methods we can find. Recognition is the first step in problem solving.

I hate to do so, but I must bring up a relatively complex subject. The subject is relativity. I know it is detrimental to put a mathematical formula in a book like this, but I have no choice. I am going to cover two theories of relativity: one is Albert Einstein's and the second is Henny Youngman's.

Einstein was a brilliant physicist and undoubtedly one of the brightest people who ever lived. His theory postulated that $E=mc^2$. His ideas were confirmed when the first atomic bomb detonated. He also postulated that everything in the universe was relative to the speed of light.

Let's explore Henny Youngman's theory of relativity. Youngman was also famous, but for a different reason. He was a comedian frequently called the king of one-liners. As an example, he said, "I'm offended by political jokes. Too often they get elected."[2] He's also responsible for my favorite by far. Responding to the question "How's your wife?" he said, "Compared to what?"[3]

His joke might sound funny, but it is a perfect example of relativity. Compared to what? My first wife, my mother, my first love who dumped me, my horse, or what? Many times, we evaluate people, experiences, likes and dislikes, and results without defining a scale of relativity.

I was at my brother's party for his seventieth birthday with three of my four siblings. I had come to the party after a visit with our father in New Hampshire. As a student of Youngman's theory of relativity, when the birthday boy asked me, "How's Dad?" I answered, "Compared to most people born in 1916, he is fabulous, but compared to how he was last year, he's not so good."

Let's assume you are a senior in high school and graduation is just a few days away. A well-meaning relative asks you, "How was your experience at your high school?" If you have gone only to that high school, you have no meaningful frame of reference. You might say your experience was good, but good compared to what? Did other schools have better facilities, fewer students, free lunches, or sharper teachers? How would you know?

Relativity also applies to likes and dislikes. I am going to get a little vulgar here, but I hope you will see the humor, and the concept might be more memorable. Going back to the line about the wife's state of being, this question might draw an interesting response. "Which do you find more pleasurable, going on a ride with your horse or with your wife?"

Unfortunately, Henny Youngman told these jokes a long time ago, and some would not work as well if the genders were reversed, so forgive me if some sound offensive in today's political climate.

My point is that if we are to examine results, we must have a method for making comparisons on a valid scale. Professional sports teams are masters at this task. Consider American football and the way teams measure the performance of players at every position. The quarterback is the most important member of the team, so teams have a quarterback-rating system that measures performance out to the tenths decimal place. You can see a great quarterback with a game rating of 158.3.[4] Teams use IQ tests to quantify the potential of prospective players to learn. Team leaders can compare prospects to others based on their competence at running, lifting weights, jumping, and other skills. Prospects must talk to sports psychologists, who evaluate their motivation and so on. Some players have violence issues, but they make their living playing football, so maybe it's okay. Athletes are continually evaluated on measurable skills (i.e., competence) and even on character. Players receive awards for outstanding community service and punishment for conduct detrimental to their sport, on and off the field.

Now for the really big question: America, how is your election system working? Let's consider the answer in terms of relativity. In a 2019 report by an independent group based at Harvard University, elections in the United States from 2012 to 2018 rated lower than those of other long-established democracies. We were ranked fifty-seventh overall. Germany was sixth, Canada was eighteenth, and France was nineteenth.[5] In a survey taken in 2016, 70% of Canadians were satisfied with their government, and only 46% of Americans were satisfied.[6] We allow a general election campaign to go on for well over a year, and Canada gets it done in under ninety days. It is a safe bet that more money is spent in one U.S. election than is spent in the combined elections of the top-twenty countries. We are not doing it on the cheap. I would also bet that the 2020 election did not raise our ranking from fifty-seventh. In my view, the ranking is right on target. The results are pathetic. When you do a cost/benefit analysis, our elections are even more pathetic.

The information about how our election system compares with that of other democracies is especially important. Very few Americans have ever lived in another country, much less experienced an election campaign in a country other than the United States. We, like the high-school student who only went to one high school, have no basis for comparison. The data above gives us a picture of where we stand. It is not pretty.

Americans, we have a problem. It is of such magnitude that small adjustments will not solve the problem. We have tried piecemeal reforms. They haven't made a dent. Some have made it worse. It's time to look at the big picture, identify the problem, and determine how to solve the problem.

I want to step back to Albert Einstein and his theory of relativity. He was definitely brilliant. He was also funny. He said, "When you are courting a nice girl, an hour seems like a second. When you sit on a red-hot cinder, a second seems like an hour. That's relativity."[7]

If you want to laugh more, look for the quotes at the end of the chapter. You will find quotes from Einstein and Youngman. They were both funny, and they were both profound. A laugh, however, will not take away the burn we should feel after the most recent elections. I felt like I was sitting on a volcano on January 6, 2021. Watching Americans assault our Capitol was terrifying.

When we acknowledge we have a problem, we've made a significant first step. We still have a long way to go. Many groups are highly invested in the current system. They will deny that a problem exists. They cannot be expected to participate in the solution in good faith.

The media thrives on the current system. It brings in billions of dollars in advertising revenue. Campaign coverage on TV looks like a reality show. What more could you ask for than a good debate where the candidates bully and verbally beat on each other? It is better than a professional wrestling match, and it's not choreographed.

Lobbyists will fight change with every dollar they can finagle from the special-interest groups they represent. The current crop of politicians will see any attempt to change the election method as a direct attack on them and on the lifestyle they enjoy. The political parties will hate to change their methods, too, because change could break the stranglehold they have on the political system. Leaders of the political parties will scream because they thrive on confrontation and power.

As a young thief, I wanted to get an engine with more horsepower and stooped to thievery. Many politicians want more horsepower, too, so they can demonstrate that they can play with the big boys. Some want to be the leader of the big boys and will go to extraordinary lengths to reach that goal. These politicians aren't interested in what they can do for our country. The character weaknesses they demonstrate are much worse than those of a ten-year-old boy. We have to give them a choice: change your ways or we will replace you with people who represent the interests of the majority of Americans.

Political party members fight each other to see which extremist view will prevail because the extremists are generally the ones who will put up the most money. Extremists resort to any tactic because they believe that the means are justified by the end. They have to win the primaries, so they attack their own team members. In the general election, they take off the gloves and really go at the opposition because they view their cause as right. They want power.

I have been telling some stories. Our politicians are great storytellers, too; however, mine are true unless otherwise stated. Unfortunately, most of their stories are less than truthful. They tell stories that they know voters want to hear. They tell voters what they think will get them elected. They have no choice. The system rewards storytellers and punishes those who dare to tell the truth. Under the current political system, candidates seeking election crave power, and only those willing to resort to what otherwise would be deplorable personal conduct have a meaningful chance to win.

═══════

If at this point you agree with the premise that we have a significant problem, I hope you will start thinking about what you can do personally. Something as easy as discussing the problem with others would help. I will present more specific ideas at the end of each chapter and at the end of the book.

Selected Quotes

"Everybody is a genius. But if you judge a fish by its ability to climb a tree, it will live its whole life believing that it is stupid."

"I have no special talents. I am only passionately curious."

"The world as we have created it is a process of our thinking. It cannot be changed without changing our thinking."

"All generalizations are false, including this one."

"Excellence is doing a common thing in an uncommon way."

"Knowledge and ego are directly related;
the less knowledge, the greater the ego."

–Albert Einstein[7]

"Who says nothing is impossible?
I've been doing nothing for years."

"A man goes to a psychiatrist.
The doctor says, 'You're crazy.'
The man says, 'I want a second opinion.'
'Okay, you're ugly, too!'"

–Henny Youngman[8]

Chapter 2

Problem Definition

"A problem well stated is a problem half solved."[1]

–John Dewey

I n this chapter, we will look at the second step in problem solving and lay the foundation to apply a problem-solving methodology to our election system. We will also discuss some subtle differences in the usage of certain terms.

In every activity, there are special words, even common words, that have distinct meanings in different contexts. If a baseball coach tells a hitter to "take" the next pitch, the hitter allows the pitch to pass the plate without swinging. If a traveler asks a train conductor how to get to his destination and is told to "take" the next train, the traveler will get on the next train. He does not let it pass.

In Chapter 1, I used the words "system" and "process" interchangeably. I will no longer do so. A system is a combination of elements to get something done. The three elements of a system are people, process, and technology. The distinction between the words becomes more important as we progress. My wife and I don't always agree; for example, we don't agree on how to wash a car. In her system, she uses a process in which she starts at the top and works down. In my system, I start at the bottom and work up. Regardless of who is doing the cleaning or the technology used, our systems differ because she uses one process and I use another. I am sure you know who has the better process and, therefore, the better system.

When designed to perform a task, a system must also take into account the environment. Let's apply that information to the story about the little thief. The task was to steal money and not get caught. The environment was the linen closet with a broken piggy bank and a house that was occasionally empty. I represented the people. Although there was no technology, the process was that I stole a few quarters at a time through a hole in the bottle. Let's now consider a hypothetical revision. Let's say that during one burglary, I cut my finger when I reached through the hole. It was a minor cut, but I worried about getting a more serious cut that would be more difficult to explain. Within my environment, in a drawer in the bathroom right next to the closet, I found tweezers. I revised my process by incorporating technology. This tool created a safer and better system, one that used all three elements of a system. Although this system was clearly basic, it was sufficient to get the job done.

Building a nuclear power plant is a good example of a complex task that requires a complex system. A project of this magnitude has to be broken down into small pieces. A big project might have thousands of systems, subsystems, and so on. Each task is basically a problem waiting for a solution. On many large construction projects, managing all of these systems requires a technique called the Critical Path Method (CPM). The objective is to make certain that each task is completed at the right time so that it does not delay the start of another task. You can't start erecting steel if the lifting equipment is not ready. You can't solve a problem until you see the problem in front of you or coming at you. Step One, then, is to realize that there is a task/problem that requires attention. The second step in problem solving is to define, clearly and accurately, the objective. Only then can a system be designed and put in place to achieve that objective.

Back to the imagined part of the little thief story. We left it at the point where the thief had stolen enough money for the motor, so he didn't need any more quarters. Let's say he went to the store and found out the cost of the motor had gone up $2.00. To make matters worse, when he went home and looked at his source of funds, he found that the hole in the bottle had been taped over and sand put in the bottom of the bottle to reduce the potential for another break in the glass. He said, "I have a problem. I have to find a way to get into the bottle without leaving a trace and get out two more dollars." The thief made a common mistake in problem solving. He focused on the wrong thing. His original problem was not that he had to find a way to get into the bottle, and it was not the problem he needed to solve now. The problem was the following: "How do I, within a short period of time, get the money to buy the motor I want?" Restating the problem opened up many more options. He could ask for a loan. He could skip lunch and save his lunch money. He could offer to mow a neighbor's lawn. The options were endless.

Here is another way to define the problem: "How can I deal with my desire to have a motor that I cannot afford?" This definition of the problem creates even more options to consider, such as buying a secondhand motor, borrowing a motor, waiting, asking for an early birthday present, shoplifting a motor, etc. This process is known as brainstorming. In brainstorming, you list every possible option and consider each one. Defining even a simple problem can be difficult, and the way you define it will determine your path and your success.

Another common error when trying to define a problem is to mistake symptoms for the problem. Symptoms are just superficial indicators that a deeper problem exists. Here is good example: I have a swimming pool, as does my neighbor. The concrete deck around her pool was cracking, so she had a contractor give her an estimate to patch it. She asked for my advice. I explained that it was unlikely a surface patch would work because the crack was probably the result of the earth settling or being eroded away. If the issue under the surface remained, the crack on the surface might reappear. She came back to me after another contractor said he could solve the problem by drilling a small hole in the concrete deck and pumping in fresh concrete to fill the void. I explained that he was getting closer to the source of the problem but still might not have reached the root cause. She was getting worried: "What's the worst it could be?" she asked. I gave her a list from bad to awful:

1. The dirt was not properly compacted, and there would be more settling.
2. There was a leak in a water line, and it was eroding the dirt.
3. A tree was cut down, and the stump, left in the ground, was rotting away, leaving a void.
4. The builder of the house dug a trash pit and covered it with earth. The trash is rotting and leaving a void.
5. Your deck is over a sinkhole.

There are many ways to define a problem. The definition will determine the best path to take to deal with the problem. The definition must not refer merely to the symptoms on the surface. Here is a sample definition: "My pool deck is cracking. The most likely cause is settlement. It would be expensive to look deeper into the problem. I will find the least expensive way to address or rule out settlement as the root cause. That might solve the problem. If not, I will have to look deeper." (All puns intended.)

Frequently, when you embark on a huge undertaking, doing it the first time is easier. Consider an old building that no longer meets current needs. You can remodel it, tear it down, and build on the same site, or you can start fresh on a new piece of land. Taking all of the potential paths into consideration affects the way you define the problem and the options available to solve the problem. Examining all of the options is a step in the problem-solving methodology that I will cover extensively later in the book. I mentioned it now because of its connection to problem definition.

Many choices rest on how you define an objective and determine the best way to achieve it. Starting with a fresh approach has resulted in numerous successful outcomes. Think about the changes that the following concepts and organizations have produced: Amazon, Tesla, Pampers, The Marshall Plan, Pringles, The Assembly Line, (Einstein's) Theory of Relativity, Turner Broadcasting, Walmart, and Apple.

I will add two names for a different reason: Ford Motors and America. Both started off with new approaches. Ford introduced the assembly line and revolutionized the automobile industry and manufacturing in general. America formed a new type of government when it revolted against Great Britain. Has either of the two made the changes they needed to keep pace with a rapidly changing world? Were they fat, dumb, and happy for too long? Did they fail to see the problems coming or not recognize the problems when they were in plain view? Were their systems incapable of dealing with these problems? Did they wait so long to take corrective measures that it might now be easier to solve some of their problems by starting from scratch?

Starting from scratch is not new to America. In 1776, we formalized our intent to separate from Great Britain when we signed the Declaration of Independence. In 1777, the Continental Congress created and signed the Articles of Confederation. They weren't ratified by all thirteen states until 1781. In 1787, our founding fathers recognized flaws in the Articles of Confederation. Leaders met to revise them but ended up scrapping them and starting over. The result was the Constitution. It was excellent, partly because it built in provisions to make changes. Changes have occurred. It is time for more changes, and big ones. Some of our systems no longer perform as well as they could and should.

Long before I was exposed to a methodical process for solving problems, I was introduced to the acronym RTP. As a student at West Point, I saw "RTP" almost every day. I saw it written on blackboards before tests. RTP stood for "Read the Problem." Too often, students gave great answers, but they were wrong because they did not address the problem they had been required to answer. This mistake exasperated the professors. One reached the point where he added a letter. It then read "RTFP." Draw your own conclusions, but I am confident that his message was "Read the Full Problem." RTP is another way of saying that problem definition and understanding are critical when searching for a workable solution.

The first part of this book is about getting things done. Problem solving and getting things done are basically the same. We all have to get things done. It could be fixing a good chicken sandwich, running a Fortune 500 corporation, or repairing an ineffective election system. The same basic techniques apply. To solve problems, you must use a methodical approach. You have to address the environment in which you operate and create systems consisting of people, technology, and process that will achieve your goals.

I have mentioned West Point and the Army. Later, I will add P&G to the mix. I will tell many stories about the time I spent working with and for those organizations. They are world-class organizations that have proven they can get things done. We have borrowed from the best. As we move on, I will get into practices, tools, and systems that have proved effective in Human Resources. These practices, tools, and systems have reduced conflict and aided in candidate screening, performance evaluation, training, and what could be referred to as "term limits." The Army has a term for what amounts to term limits: "Up or Out." If you can't move up in rank, you are moved out to make room for others with more potential. P&G has a term for it too: "termination." West Point calls it "dismissal." All three organizations have excellent means for measuring performance, one of the most important being comparative merit based on results.

I have used the words "circumstances" and "environment," and these words are interchangeable. Let's return to the pool deck problem and demonstrate how the circumstances can change the way we deal with a problem. My neighbor and I live in Atlanta. Georgia is known for its red clay. It can be compacted easily, and it does not erode as quickly as black soil. Let's theoretically move our houses to Florida, which is known for its sandy soil and sinkholes. If our neighbor a block away just had his house devoured by a sinkhole, our situation will seem much more precarious.

In Florida or Georgia, if the deck problem occurred thirty-five years ago, the only way to get below the concrete slab would be to break it up and check out the problem. Today, we can make a tiny hole in the concrete, put a miniature camera through the hole, and take a look. We have technology and process to incorporate into our problem solving that were not available in the past. Too frequently, when trying to solve a problem, we ignore new technology or use it only to give us more of what people did before. In many cases, this approach just increases the cost without changing the outcome. Sometimes, we fail to see that the technology could be a game-changer for the better if we took full advantage of its capabilities and made appropriate changes in the people and processes making up the system.

In the early 1970s, I was the mechanical department manager in a warehouse in Cincinnati. The warehouse was part of a P&G complex called Ivorydale. Three manufacturing plants were in the complex, plus a warehouse that stored and shipped all of the goods produced by the three plants. The plants made bar soap, laundry detergent, and toothpaste. My first assignment at P&G had been in the detergent plant. At that time, all product had to be loaded on trucks and transported to the warehouse, where they were then unloaded. There had to be a better way to move the boxes to the warehouse, and P&G solved the problem.

P&G designed an elaborate conveyor system to move all of the boxes from the plants to the warehouse. One section of the system went over a wide roadway and across a big parking lot. This section of the system had to be one continuous belt, and at that time, it was the longest continuous conveyor belt in the world. My department was responsible for maintaining that system. Three machinists and three electricians were assigned to this task. The belts ran twenty-four hours a day, five days a week. When I started this assignment, the technicians were dealing with a problem that the engineers had not anticipated. Four belts carried the boxes. The housing for the four belts was a bridge that looked like an enclosed pedestrian walkway. Two belts, like bunk beds, were on each wall, with a walkway down the middle. Safety regulations required a means to warn people who might be near or working on a belt when it was starting up. The engineers used a fairly common technique. They placed horns throughout the bridge. When a belt started running, the horns blared. The solution sounded good, but it didn't work.

The engineers didn't realize the amount of noise that would be generated by the thousands of rollers moving at one time and the boxes bumping along. If three belts were running and the fourth belt was being restarted, workers couldn't hear the horns. My guys had not read their Einstein: "We cannot solve our problems with the same thinking we used when we created them."[2]

My electricians wanted to order more and louder horns to solve the problem because they defined the problem as needing more noise to overcome the noise. I redefined the problem in this way: We need a better method to warn people that a belt is restarting. When I took into consideration the environment, I saw the light, literally. The best way to warn people was to install flashing lights.

In another assignment at P&G, I operated out of the internal audit department. I worked at corporate headquarters as a specialist in security because I had extensive security experience in the Army. I had commanded a unit that maintained a nuclear weapon storage facility and later became an inspector who checked on eight nuclear weapon storage sites. I also had a security job in Vietnam and was the operations officer at a school where all classes were classified "Secret." We had bars and alarms everywhere.

My role at P&G was unusual because I had two masters. I was on loan from the manufacturing division to the comptroller's division. My boss from manufacturing was the division manager of the Ivorydale complex. My boss in the comptroller's division was the department head of internal auditing. A feud was going on between manufacturing and the security group. The manufacturing group thought the security department was doing the manufacturing group more harm than good.

My two bosses were in a "friendly" conflict. They saw a problem—discord between the security group and the manufacturing side of the company—but they didn't understand the reasons for the friction. I replaced the previous person on loan from manufacturing who had the title of corporate security coordinator. Just as I had two bosses, I had two roles. The way my predecessor handled those two roles was the source of conflict.

As corporate security coordinator, I provided security expertise on all matters connected to the protection of company assets. The assets included people, physical and intellectual property, and image. One major problem we were dealing with was the spreading of false rumors about the P&G trademark, which we referred to as "the moon and stars." Rumormongers claimed the trademark was a satanic symbol and that the company was in league with the devil. That image was not the one P&G wanted to present to millions of customers around the world.

QAnon, part of the group that stormed the Capitol on January 6, 2021, is not as creative as one might think. Many others have claimed a link between their opponents and the devil.

A few years before I moved into the security job, a disgruntled marketing manager stole the marketing plan for Crest toothpaste. He offered to sell it to Colgate Palmolive, a major competitor. Colgate was a tough competitor, but it had integrity. It contacted the FBI. What happened would make good television. The thief and the representative from Colgate went into adjoining stalls in a bathroom at JFK Airport. They exchanged briefcases under the common wall of the stalls. The Colgate man then had the marketing plan and the thief had the money. The thief was not as good as I was at age ten. Briefcase in hand, he walked into the waiting arms of an FBI agent, who arrested him for stealing trade secrets. Indeed, the marketing plan had previously been stamped "secret." My group established the procedures that protected intellectual property. These two situations give you an idea about one of my roles.

I also had to visit all of the company's manufacturing plants in the United States and Canada. I had to ensure the plants followed company policy and procedure with regard to security and discuss any local security issues. My predecessor made these visits unannounced and liked to play "stealth ninja." He found a way to sneak into the plant at night, a task not hard to accomplish if you are a determined aggressor because a comprehensive security system would have been cost prohibitive. The next morning, he met with the local security manager and explained how bad the security system was and how much damage he could have caused. To further ingratiate himself, he wrote a report on the results of his visit and sent it to the plant manager, the division manager, and the vice president of all manufacturing. As you might expect, when a plant security manager later could have used expert advice, he refused to contact the security department. The saying comes to mind, "I am from the government, and I'm here to help."

I could not accomplish my two roles using the process in place. You cannot embarrass someone one day and expect him to come to you the next day to ask for help, especially if that person perceives you as an SOB who is trying to make himself look good by making you look bad.

I went to the Internal Auditing Department head and suggested some changes. There would be no more unannounced visits. "Ninja" attacks were out. I would go to manufacturing facilities to review their security and provide a "consulting" service. I persuaded my boss to agree with the changes I proposed, with one exception. I still had to prepare a report on each visit. He let me scale back on the distribution, but not as much as I wanted. I dealt with that issue by being selective about what I put in my visit reports and watching the tone I used. I was there to help, and I conducted myself that way throughout the visit. I conveyed that same message in the reports. Only if I encountered serious problems and an unwillingness to cooperate did I use the clout that can come with being from corporate headquarters.

Problem solving is best done with a methodical approach. Step One is to recognize that you have a problem. Step Two is to dig and dig until you have found the root causes. Great care must be taken to ensure that results and symptoms are not incorrectly viewed as the problem. We can easily make mistakes if we only put a patch on a problem, as in the pool-deck situation.

Doing more of the same thing is frequently not the best solution, as in the conveyor-belt story.

Changes to the environment can change everything. We must make sure we include these changes in our definition, as in the little-thief and pool-deck cases.

Conflict is the enemy of progress, and it can be a contributing factor that has to be identified and resolved as part of solving a problem, as in the corporate security coordinator job.

The most effective tactics involve brainstorming and borrowing from the best.

Most importantly, if you have been fat, dumb, and happy too long and you have placed patch on top of patch, it might be best to create a whole new system.

Defining problems has parallels to defining beauty. To make a determination on either one, you have to take a close look. If this book stimulates you to take a look at what is going on in politics and you agree it is ugly, you can put your definition on it and make a decision about the severity of the problem. Based on that decision, you might choose to ask others to look at the problem, just as you might ask neighbors to examine a vacant lot that you think is hurting the value of your home and other homes near it. The lot might be so ugly in your view that you try to get a group together to fix the mess. That's why I am writing this book. I am hoping I can convince readers to take a close look at the mess we are in and join an effort to get it fixed.

Selected Quotes[3]

"If I had an hour to solve a problem, I'd spend fifty-five minutes thinking about the problem and five minutes thinking about the solution."

–Albert Einstein

"Understand the exact nature of the problem. Understanding of the issue if faulty; your attempt to resolve it will also be flawed."

–Santosh Chadha

"When you gain certainty about a problem, the problem is solved."

–Meir Ezra

Chapter 3

Circumstances/Environment

"Do something. If it works, do more of it. If it doesn't, do something different." [1]

–Franklin D. Roosevelt

I n Chapter 2, we looked at a small problem involving a cracked swimming pool deck. We changed the circumstances and saw how changing the circumstances altered the way we needed to define and possibly solve the problem.

Let's look at a sampling of the changes that have occurred from the time we became self-governing to now. Some are broad in scope, such as the best way to get anything done, and some are narrow, such as how to collect votes. By necessity, this chapter is the longest in the book and the most challenging to get through. You might decide to read some of it more than once.

Our circumstances are vastly different from what they were 230 years ago. Because prevailing circumstances determine how we solve the problems of today, it is important to take everything that has changed into consideration. Changes have upsides and down-sides. Automobiles have revolutionized travel, but they result in serious accidents, require the expenditure of billions of dollars to maintain road networks, and cause air pollution. This change, like health care and many others, must be managed to maximize the positives and minimize the negatives. We can do better than we have in the last fifty years.

In the late 1940s, the world was adjusting to the consequences of World War II. The Allies won the war, but every country except for the United States was a loser. Germany had 6.9 million dead and 7.3 million wounded. The country was split into four zones, and the zone to the east would become a satellite of the Soviet Union. Germany's infrastructure and production facilities had been reduced to rubble, as had many residences. The country was flooded with displaced people. The Soviet Union, still trying to prove that communism could work, had 20 million dead.

Japan had 2.5 million dead and had been heavily bombed, in-cluding the only two atomic bombs ever dropped on metropolitan areas.

China had 15 million dead and was in a civil war, a war that the communists would win.

Great Britain had 451,000 dead and had suffered heavy damage from German bombs and rockets. The combined total of deaths for other European countries was over 10 million.

American deaths numbered 419,400, with sixteen countries ahead of the United States.[2] Rather than have our production ca-pabilities reduced or destroyed, however, American industrial capacity was far greater than it had been before the war. The American economy was exploding, and the war had lifted us out of the Depression. With the economies of major countries around the world shattered, America was king of the hill.

As the world began rebuilding, an open-minded problem

solver tried to sell new ideas to American industrialists about how to get things done. He made the rounds without much success. He called on automobile manufacturers. They viewed his ideas as "way out" and saw no reason to make the dramatic changes he suggested. Why should they? Business was booming, and firms were making a fortune. They didn't take into consideration that there was no competition beyond other American car companies. No one seemed worried about what might happen when countries like Germany and Japan got back on their feet.

Our problem solver took his ideas to Japan. There he was met with a great deal of interest. Manufacturers were almost starting from scratch, so they could more easily implement new ideas. Workers were amiable to any conditions, as long as they earned a living. The result was an automobile industry revolution that put some American car companies into bankruptcy and reshaped the auto industry around the world. American car companies are still playing catch-up. The revolution reshaped many ideas about the right type of culture for productive organizations. Culture is part of the circumstances we will examine.

The problem solver was Dr. W. Edwards Deming. His revolutionary idea is simple to state but hard to implement: We get better results if we work together than if we work against each other.

Try explaining that concept and selling it to U.S. politicians. Many of them have spent their entire adult lives fighting others. They were elected because they were better at fighting than compromising and playing nicely with others. The culture they thrive in is one of conflict.

My first in-depth exposure to Deming's ideas came when I began working for P&G in 1970. At that time, P&G called the concept "Democracy in Industry." It would later become known as "Total Quality Management" (TQM). It was also referred to as "TQM/Continuous Improvement" because improvement is the never-ending goal. I will use TQM. We were trying to change the culture of a large industrial complex in Cincinnati. Many of the hourly employees and some managers were second and third-generation employees. If they went home after a training session on TQM principles and told their dads or granddads about it, the elders would say something like, "They expect you to do *what*? Don't let 'em get away with it. They're out to screw you and make more money for themselves." TQM met with heavy resistance. Deming's idea that much better performance would occur if management and labor worked with one another and not against each other turned out to be very difficult to implement in the culture in place.

P&G found that the best method to implement TQM was to go to a rural area, build a new plant, and staff it with managers that had been trained in TQM. Those managers then hired the workforce and ensured it would largely consist of people who had never worked in a manufacturing environment before so that they couldn't compare their work environment at P&G with any other. They had no built-in resistance to TQM. There was no relativity. To them, TQM was what it was like to work in manufacturing. They were happy to have a job where they were paid well and treated well. They felt they were an important part of a team working together to achieve goals that were good for all.

I devote a later chapter to TQM. I mention it here because it is one of the major changes that have taken place in the last seventy-five years. When we take an in-depth look at our election system, TQM will provide a significant framework for defining the problem and striving to fix a very flawed system. TQM is a new tool in our tool chest, just as the miniature TV camera was in the cracked-concrete-deck situation.

Let's travel back in time again, this time to 1919. It is the aftermath of what we now refer to as World War I. Before World

War II, World War I was called "The Great War," and to some optimists, it was the "war to end all wars." The German Empire, Austro-Hungarian Empire, and others of the Central Powers were defeated by the allied countries. The Allied Forces won the war but lost the peace.[3] The Treaty of Versailles saddled Germany, in particular, with a loss of territory, heavy reparations, and guilt. The outcome for the Germans and Austrians was economic collapse. It took only twenty years for this situation to produce Adolph Hitler and the next world war.

We can be thankful that after World War II, another American had outside-the-box ideas. Dr. Deming was just starting to spread his ideas when George Marshall came to similar conclusions. He looked at the results of the peace after World War I and said, "Let's not repeat history. Rather than punish our enemies and collect the spoils of war, the tradition going back for centuries, why don't we help them and turn them into our friends? In fact, helping them might be in our best interests because we reduce the potential for future hostilities and create customers we will need if we are going to grow our economy." His concept became known as "The Marshall Plan."[4]

Secretary of State and Secretary of Defense George C. Marshall, an Army general and a confidant of President Franklin D. Roosevelt, was also a Nobel Peace Prize Laureate. He recognized that circumstances had changed. We needed a different approach. Isolation was no longer an option. We were the major economic and military power in the world. It was becoming obvious that our World War I and World War II ally, the Soviet Union, was becoming our worst enemy. It was spreading its communist culture around the world and was willing to resort to force, which included a nuclear arsenal. Within twenty years, the Soviet Union and China, both former allies, were opponents, and our former enemies, Germany, Japan, and Italy, were our friends. That's a big change!

I see little need to elaborate on changes that go back even further, such as spreading from the Atlantic to the Pacific, expanding to fifty states from thirteen, freeing the slaves after a brutal civil war, and finally recognizing in 1920 that women deserve the right to be full partners in our democracy.

Now we will look at changes more directly connected to politics and, more specifically, to our election system. I will group them together under four broad headings you should find familiar: systems, people, technology, and process.

Systems and process are closely linked, both being ways to get things done. I use the term "process" to connect people and technology in the accomplishment of a task. A system is the combination of all three elements. Finding a process that has undergone change without an accompanying change in either people or technology is difficult. In most cases, the technology has changed. In some cases, changes are interconnected and do not neatly fit in a single category.

As you review these many areas of change and the consequences, think about the divide caused by using an idealistic approach to a situation instead of a pragmatic approach. A change that is "good" from an idealistic viewpoint might be "bad" from a pragmatic view. And the reverse is also true.

Systems

We are going to examine several systems. The first is education. It is extraordinarily important so it gets lots of attention. But, all the systems covered contributed to our current predicament, and how we manage them will have a major impact on our future.

Education

The essence of TQM is that working together is much better than working against one another. You must change to improve, and what you reap is a function of the system you have in place. Our educational system has changed, but has it changed enough?

Albert Einstein made the following observations:[5]
- "We cannot solve our problems with the same *thinking* we used when we created them."
- "Peace cannot be kept by force; it can be achieved only by *understanding*."
- "Two things are infinite: the universe and human *stupidity*, and I'm not sure about the universe."

I have experienced a good bit of stupidity in my lifetime, especially when I was young. I was a participant in activities I now question. I have been in a war zone. I was at the Berlin wall before and after it came down. I was responsible for escorting refugees from East Germany to processing centers after they crawled through minefields to reach the West. I was the property officer for more than a dozen nuclear weapons and taught soldiers how to assemble and place them where they would do the most "good" to stop an invading army. Einstein was brilliant. He recognized how vital education is. Thinking, understanding, and stupidity are all functions of education.

I come from a family of educators, and my path was no different. In the Army, I learned formal teaching and taught nuclear weapons assembly. Our military services are among the biggest and best teaching/training organizations in the world. They teach construction work, such as building bridges. Military personnel maintain and operate nuclear-powered ships and maintain and fly airplanes. Many commercial pilots learned how to fly in our armed services. After I left the Army, I entered a training program at P&G. I was going to be a guinea big for a new training concept:

Objective-Oriented Training (OOT). This program gave me even more appreciation for the U.S. Army. My last assignment in the army was as a supervisor of instructors training soldiers to assemble nuclear weapons. We used OOT.

OOT has a lot in common with TQM. In both, you define what you want to accomplish in measurable terms. You then establish a system to accomplish the task, such as training an airplane pilot to fly in all types of weather, take off and land on an aircraft carrier, and handle malfunctions such as engine failure. Each phase of instruction starts with an objective, and a system is created to achieve that objective. At the end of each phase, the student must demonstrate that he has reached the goal by performing tasks that are objectively measurable.

Education is more critical than ever in today's world. Almost everything is more complicated than in the past. Many unintended consequences can arise from what appears to be an easy solution. You need to be educated, but not brainwashed, to make good choices on an election ballot. You need to know a little history so that you know when a proposal hasn't worked in previous attempts. You should be able to rule out idealistic objectives if they are impractical. You have to have some ability to distinguish between facts, beliefs, and bovine manure. In the political arena, especially around election time, facts are scarce.

Education has changed, but were the changes good or not so good? Did we make the big changes that we should have made? Did we change too slowly? Did we take into consideration changes such as America having shifted from an agricultural economy to an industrial economy? Have we factored in the rise in divorce rates, families having fewer children, our population becoming more diverse, and the advent of two-wage-earner families? Could we merge our educational system with another system (e.g., our armed forces) and realize benefits in two or more areas?

Before giving you my rationale for these questions, as well as some answers, I need to differentiate between recommendations and options. My answers are options. They are not recommendations. Part of problem solving under TQM is brainstorming. You let everyone involved in solving the problem put out any option they can think of, and dismiss no option immediately. Elimination of options occurs only after there are no more to add to the list. The first option to eliminate is the worst on the list, and you work your way through those remaining. Sometimes two options have no appeal individually but, when combined, form a new and great option. The best options become recommendations. And brainstormers should not lose sight of relativity. If there are no good options, the best of the bad options might still be a lot better than the option of doing nothing.

My sister-in-law was a teacher in Maryland, as was my brother. When the No Child Left Behind law was passed in 2001,[6] she wanted to retire as soon as possible. The law had many provisions, but the two that frustrated her to tears were the placement of children with disabilities, including learning disabilities, and non-English-speaking-children in regular classrooms. It might have been idealistically good, but from a pragmatic standpoint, it was awful. A teacher had to spend much more time with special-needs children, to the detriment of other students. A law intended to improve education had two significant consequences that diminished its effectiveness. Dedicated but frustrated teachers left teaching, and the pace of learning slowed for the majority of students.

I attended my brother's retirement ceremony. The principal who had hired him and had himself retired was present, along with the current principal. My brother told me that he had a fine relationship with the old principal but that he and the new principal had different philosophies of teaching and didn't get along.

The new principal's philosophy was that students should be told repeatedly that they can do or be anything they set their mind to and work hard enough to achieve. My brother's philosophy was that every child has an aptitude for and ability to do certain things and that the job of educators is to help students find their best path and equip them to succeed on that path. Furthermore, my brother felt that the "you can be anything" approach led to a rude awakening for many students when they were in their early teens and arrived at the conclusion that they had been misled. For some, their school experience went downhill from there. How could such directly opposed positions exist? You would think that educators would research the issue, determine an answer, and get everyone on the same page.

We made an attempt to improve education, but it was not nearly soon enough. Neither did it address much bigger and problematic issues. To complicate matters further, it mixed idealistic goals with a pragmatic attempt to improve education.

My son has been a teacher at the college level for more than twenty years. He has taught in Illinois and Georgia at four schools. He believes our educational system is badly broken. Many of his students are unprepared to perform at the college level. He and his colleagues are frustrated because they want to see their students pass their classes, but only about 50% can make the grade. Worse is the frustration students experience because they were led to believe they were ready for college. They do well in high school but are failing in college. Many of the failing students and their parents blame the college professors.

Misled students who move from high school to college can become frustrated and angry adults. They might blame anyone but themselves, and, in a way, they are right. The system is to blame. The system steered them down a path, toward college, that was wrong for them. They would have been better off placed in programs that trained them in a field for which they had an aptitude and interest. Plumbing, welding, and many other professions are equally or more lucrative than many professions that require a college degree.

Part of the problem in the United States is that people without a college degree are generally disrespected. In Germany, a much smaller percentage of children are put on a path to college—only those who have demonstrated the interest and the aptitude. Their college education will be paid for by the state. Those not going to college go to trade schools that turn out highly skilled, well paid, and respected professionals. My wife, educated in Germany, is a professional dressmaker. She worked at a fashion house making clothes for models. She can look at a dress in a magazine, make a pattern for it, and make the dress. The son of a friend went to school to be a waiter. He liked his work and was good at what he did. Last we knew, he was a *maître d'* at an exclusive restaurant. The German system of education is geared toward the interest and ability of each student. Perhaps we could borrow some ideas from it.

Let's look at the big picture, the results of our system. Keep in mind that the results are not the problem. They are like the cracks in the concrete deck. We have to dig deeper, down to the flaws in the system, before we can fix the problem.

In 2020 and 2021, we had an appalling presidential election and transition of power. Recent elections have shown a digression away from civility that is troubling. It seems we have lost sight of who we are as a people and how things are supposed to happen in a democracy. Across the board, there has been a shift away from independent, level-headed thinking and even the pretense of trying to be understanding. And there has clearly been enough stupidity to capture worldwide interest. Our educational system is partly to blame.

Education has an impact on everything we do or try to do, so I've spent a great deal of time on the subject in a broad sense. Now I will move quickly through some of the specific questions I raised.

The current school year is similar to what was in place when the bulk of Americans were farmers. They needed their children to work on the farm in the summer. Because America is now more industrially based, should we consider a school year that runs year-round? Students could learn more, we could use those expensive school facilities year-round, we could pay teachers more, and we could offer full-year, after-school programs that help parents pursue their careers.

My older brother taught new teachers after he retired from teaching high school. Many of his students were making a career change from industry to teaching. A student came to him after class and asked for advice on how he could get his teenage daughter back on track in school. She had lost interest and her grades were dropping. My brother asked one question: "Have you recently gone through a divorce?" The student said, "Yes." Do we have enough special guidance counseling for children suffering through parental divorce?

We have smaller families and more single-parent homes. When two parents are present, both are usually wage earners. What's the impact on our educational system?

My paternal grandmother, Rosa, came to America in 1903 from a city in Russia nicknamed the dressmaking capital of Europe. Russia, then and now, has an excellent educational system. She was taught to be a professional seamstress. In America, she started her own business making clothes and doing alterations. She did so well that she was able to buy a house. After her husband was killed in an accident, she was able to support her family, even during the Great Depression.

Today, many American children have parents who came from countries with poor educational systems. The lack of education makes it harder for parents and children to rise from poverty and participate in a complicated democratic system. Some who come here are intent on undermining our way of life and spreading dangerous beliefs. The poorly educated are most susceptible because they are unemployed or under employed, a condition that alienates them and keeps them at poverty level. They are unable to understand and accept their misfortune. They are easily convinced that they deserve better and that violence is justified.

When we ended the military draft in 1973,[7] we did what most young people considered a good deed. But as the saying goes, "No good deed goes unpunished." The draft was seriously flawed, and we should never return to the system used in the past. However, the draft had some very positive consequences. It put young people into an excellent educational system. For many, it turned a bleak future into a brighter one. Not only did these people receive formal and on-the-job training, but they were also sent to distant places and exposed to different cultures and new ideas. Many stayed in the service and had a good career. Many took advantage of the benefits and went back to school. Most matured into more responsible and productive adults. For some it was a path to citizenship. We should take the positive aspects of having young adults serve their country and create a system that benefits both the individual and the country. Many countries have such systems. I will discuss my ideas along these lines later in the book.

Einstein talked about changing our thinking, striving for understanding, and overcoming stupidity. All three fall under the heading of education. Education and progress are almost synonymous. If a country wants to have a better election system, or a populace that can make continuous improvements, it needs a great education system.

Entitlements

Ida Fuller was one lucky woman. In 1940, she was the first regular recipient of a Social Security check. She was sixty-five and had paid $22.54 into Social Security. At a time when life expectancy was about sixty-two years, she lived to be one hundred and collected $22,888.92 in benefits.[8] She represented the early start of "entitlement" programs that reshaped the federal government and its role in America. The thinking that went into Social Security was reasonable at the time, although it mimicked a Ponzi scheme. Ida Fuller's payments came from those in the workforce after her, those not ready to collect benefits. If life expectancy remained at sixty-two and payments didn't start until age sixty-five, everything would have been fine. However, a few circumstances changed. Life expectancy is now seventy-nine years.[9] In addition, it's possible to start receiving Social Security benefits as early as age sixty-two, and even earlier if you're disabled.

Medicare came on the scene in 1966.[10] It was intended to provide funds for medical care for people over sixty-five. Almost sixty years later, we have many modern miracles of medicine that were probably not on anyone's radar in 1966. I am old and have old friends. Two receive treatment for a serious medical condition. One refers to himself as the Million Dollar Man because of the annual cost of his treatments. The other man has him beat. His treatment is $100,000 a month. We want the federal government to provide benefits and handle all of the associated administrative details, but we don't want to have the costs passed on to us taxpayers, and we don't want a government employee making life-and-death decisions for us. Those preferences are only feasible in the long term if we are very productive and willing to share some of the fruits of our productivity with people who require help.

Entitlements and other government costs play a major role in every election. Each side makes the same claims to voters: "I will give you more for less, and my opponent will raise your taxes and waste your money." Those claims have worked so well that our national debt is 22 trillion dollars and is increasing at an alarming rate.[11]

Non-Military Wars

We tried an interesting experiment in 1919. We passed the prohibition amendment that banned the manufacture, sale, and transportation of liquor. It was idealism run amuck. It didn't stop people from drinking. Instead, it increased illegal activity and made criminals filthy rich. Bootleggers had no difficulty finding customers. Many Americans didn't want to change their drinking habits. As evidence, Henny Youngman later joked, "When I read about the evils of drinking, I gave up reading."[12]

It took until 1933 for more pragmatic people to overturn that amendment. What a waste! Those fourteen years did much more harm than good. The worst part is that we didn't learn from that experience that the government can only do so much and that we need to take care in picking the wars we choose to fight.

We have had our share of military conflicts since 1919, and we have also entered into wars on poverty, drugs, homelessness, energy dependence, and more. Part of problem solving is prioritizing. Later, we will talk about Franklin D. Roosevelt, a master at prioritizing.

Think of the timing of Amendment XVIII, Prohibition. World War I had just ended, women had not yet been granted the right to vote, and we pushed through an amendment to spare the country from the evils of alcohol. Prohibition was only the eighth change we had made to the Constitution in 130 years, not counting the first ten amendments, the Bill of Rights, which were part of the original document.

Political Parties

George Washington, as he was retiring from politics, warned us about the potential problems that political parties could cause. We now have two dominant political parties that stifle independent thinking and champion conflict rather than teamwork. They routinely prevent their opposition from doing things that need to be done to keep the opposition from looking good. Worse, we have what I call the "doing and undoing." These reversals in major undertakings are usually connected to the ideals of the two parties. It is not the same as undoing Prohibition, which was clearly a failure and could not be fixed. Two good examples of doing and undoing are government health insurance and the wall along our border with Mexico. These turnarounds are tied to value differences related to the role of the federal government and patriotism.

We keep going back and forth because we have no clear direction. The party system pushes us toward extremes. If the politicians we put in office were more representative of moderate Americans and less combative, we might be able to agree on a direction and more pragmatically pursue a consistent course of action. When there is a political party change in the White House, the first thing the new president does is undo what his predecessor has done. Doing and then undoing accomplishes nothing. It is worse than doing nothing. It squanders time and resources.

Polling

Poll taking is a new system that could not exist without modern technology. Pollsters determine what voters want to hear. Speechwriters use that information to write speeches that will win votes. The polling information even allows politicians to modify their messages as they travel from place to place to win the favor of voters with differing views. Polls are very much a part of the win-at-any-cost mentality of politicians and their parties.

Special-Interest Groups

Special-interest groups and their paid lobbyists are also relatively new. To compete in politics, big money is essential. The more a special-interest group has at stake, the more money it will pay lobbyists to work toward a desirable outcome. It's another element of the win-at-any-cost mindset. Special-interest groups don't care whether something is good for the majority of Americans. What matters is that the group *believes* it is best for everyone or at least for themselves and their brethren, often without proof. Special-interest groups number in the hundreds. Some might have ideals that are good, but all have their own agenda.

People

No system will work well unless the right people are the performers within the system and are the managers of the system. Their character, capabilities, and expectations must be considered when determining the objective of a system and its design.

Attitude

People haven't changed much, but their attitudes have changed, as have the circumstances that affect expectations. Many Americans have grown up in a society dependent on government systems. But many Americans don't understand what it takes to provide these services or the tradeoffs that come with every government-provided benefit. Few can remember when families were responsible for parents and grandparents. One reason people had children was to have someone who would take care of them in their old age. Serious health issues went untreated when there was no family, the family couldn't raise the money to provide necessary medical care, or no charitable organization was willing to help. Today, most Americans not only take medical benefits for granted, they demand them.

Part of the downside of some of our benefits programs and the way we administer them is that they influence the laws of supply and demand. Take my seventy-year-old friend whose medication costs $100,000 a month. Medication that costs $100,000 a month would not be on the market if there were no demand. How many individuals or families could bear the cost of such care? The answer is not enough. The cost/benefit analysis doesn't work. We deal with this by passing the cost on to a third party that then transfers the cost to future generations. That is part of the reason our debt is so high and growing rapidly. We have manipulated the demand.

The last fifty years have also seen a major change in the psychology of raising children. When I was a child, my parents made it clear by word and deed that "children were to be seen and not heard." My parents loved and cared for me, but I was not the center of their universe. The philosophy today is summed up in the expression a new father recently used: "Children are our future." I felt like saying, "No sh*t!" That fact, however, doesn't mean we should spoil them and lead them to believe that their welfare and happiness comes before that of all others. The result is many adults who focus on what is best for themselves and their children rather than the common good. They rant and rave about their individual rights while collecting from others all they can get. They see no relationship between rights and obligations. It is analogous to an individual who expects a sibling to send a birthday card with a hundred-dollar bill inside each year but feels imposed upon if the sibling asks for a few hours of babysitting help.

Complexity

Because of the complexity of today's world, we need to rely on the knowledge and opinions of experts, yet many Americans listen only to advice from folks whose views are more palatable to them. The 2020-2021 pandemic is a case in point. Most experts recommended that we take precautions such as wearing face masks and maintaining physical distance from others. Many Americans still refuse to acknowledge and comply with this advice because it "violates their individual rights." With all of the various news forums available today, finding an "expert" who supports your view and allows you to justify your actions is easy.

Haves vs. Have-Nots

Over the years, the gap between the wealthy and the poor has widened. It will continue to do so unless we come to grips with the causes. Our education system is one of the major causes. Americans must gain the knowledge and skills to compete in a world filled with competent people. They must learn the importance of productivity, be capable of being productive, and adopt an attitude consistent with productivity. It takes knowledge, competence, and good character to be a productive part of a complex society.

Technology

Changes in technology have enabled us to get things done in ways no one could have conceived 230 years ago. We have sent men to the moon and brought them back, constructed ships that sail under water for months, and can transfer the heart of a dead person into a living one to extend a life. We can calculate in seconds mathematical equations that took years to calculate before digital computers. We have robots that produce complicated products faster, better, and cheaper than human beings. And the rate of technological change is steadily accelerating.

Technology can be used for good or bad. The technology we use to get things done, such as inform voters about candidates and hold fair elections, is no different. It is within our capability to derive more good than bad if the technology is part of a well-constructed system. I will focus on only five areas of technological change that have a direct bearing on politics and elections: transportation, communications, digital computers, social media, and voting.

Transportation

In 1789, when our Constitution became the law of the land, the fastest mode of travel was the horse. A rider willing and able to stay in the saddle for eight hours a day could cover about thirty-two miles. A rider could go from New York City to Ohio in two weeks. It took five weeks to go from New York City to Illinois. By 1830, the train was the quickest way to travel, but it was still a two-week trip from New York City to Illinois. By 1930, trains were faster.[13] You could travel from New York City to California in four days. Commercial airplanes came on the scene in the 1940s, and trips that once took eight weeks then took eight hours. Apply these changes in transportation to the process of campaigning for elections. Although the country expanded across the continent, by the 1930s, a politician could get on a train and make a whistle-stop campaign across the country in a week. Add in helicopters and airplanes, and a Washington-based politician in 2020 could be in ten major cities in a day. Abraham Lincoln had difficulty getting the same thing done in ten days. Obviously, transportation has improved over the years.

Communications

Those pursuing elected office have always had to get their message out to the electorate. They needed to get in front of the people and say who they were and what they planned to accomplish if elected. Terms commonly used included "stumping" and "getting on a soapbox" because politicians stood on a tree stump or got on a soapbox to deliver their message. They attended town hall meetings, slapped the flesh (shook hands), and kissed babies to ingratiate themselves with voters. Modern forms of communication replaced those necessities.

Today, politicians use TV, email, tweets, and videos to deliver their messages. Shaking hands and kissing babies can be dangerous for politicians, as evidenced by what happened to George

Wallace, Robert Kennedy, and Gabby Gifford. In 1960, I went to see John F. Kennedy on his whistle-stop tour on Long Island. I never got within a hundred feet of him and could barely hear a word he said. I had to climb a pole to get a glimpse of him. I doubt that a train-station encounter such as mine was helpful for anyone in attendance in selecting a president. (As an aside, in June of 1962, President Kennedy walked directly in front of me on the parade field at West Point. He arrived by helicopter to make the graduation speech. I was in the front line of the honor guard there to greet him. This time I was within a couple feet of him. Our picture appeared on the front page of a New York newspaper. The photo appears at the end of this chapter.)

Digital Computers

Computers came into general use in the 1960s. Among other things, they made us capable of collecting and analyzing tremendous amounts of data. Weather forecasting is an example. Without computers, reasonably accurate hour-by-hour predictions of temperature and rainfall would be impossible. Computers allow us to monitor billions of electronic messages and screen them for keywords that could alert us to an impending terrorist attack. Politicians use computers to make plans or promises that maximize their election potential. They focus their efforts where they will do the most good for them. They focus their time and advertising dollars on geographic areas where they can shift enough critical votes to produce a win where most needed.

Social Media

Social media is one of the newest and most impactful changes in our society. It could be considered one of the changes in communications, but it so new and distinct from radio and TV that I put it in a special category. It has been around for only about twenty years. Today, many Americans get their news through social media, allowing anyone with internet access to spread a message to millions of other people with internet access. The message might not be truthful or logical. Some messages might be comparable to screaming "Fire!" when there is no fire. Some are messages of hate. Donald Trump was the first president to harness the full power of social media.

Voting

Technology has also changed the way votes are collected and counted. Originally, voters wrote the name of their preferred candidate on a slip of paper and put it in a box. Later, ballots were printed, many in newspapers. Around 1910, mechanical voting machines came into use. Voters flipped manual levers to enter their votes, and the machine helped in the counting process.[14] Next came electronic voting, bringing computers into the mix, but we still go to polling places to vote and the counting process can be a nightmare.

Politicians are not the only things people vote for these days. Some TV shows invite viewers to pick their favorites. Shows can count the votes and determine a winner in twenty-four hours.

Much like our entire election system, our voting system started more than two hundred years ago. We have modified it many times. It has become a hodgepodge of activities that strains the definition of "system." Perhaps it's time to drop the thinking that put us where we are and use every tool available to invent a new system.

Process

In a system, process links people and technology to accomplish a task, whether simple or complex. The system must be appropriate for the prevailing conditions. A better process might come about using new ideas or it might be connected to new technology or new attitudes held by the people involved.

Length of Campaigns

In the 2016 presidential race, the campaign ran for 596 days.[15] The clock starts running when a candidate officially files an application to run. On January 20, 2017, Donald Trump filed papers to run in 2020,[16] almost four years before the election. Many potential candidates campaign continually for election or reelection. I doubt the elections in the 1800s took more than a year. If your objective is to have an efficient, effective election system, it makes no sense for campaigns to go on for years. Only the media benefits when the process drags out for such long periods.

Money Raising

Running for national office takes a great deal of money. Raising the funds is a critical element of the process. Some attempts have been made to address fundraising problems, without much success. In 1976, it became possible for presidential candidates to get funding from taxpayers,[17] but as with most gifts, conditions applied. Barak Obama was considered a master at organizing a political machine and raising money. He chose not to use government funds, I assume, because he didn't need them and didn't want to comply with the accompanying conditions. But did his ability to build an organization and raise money demonstrate the competence and character we need in a president? The same question applies to Donald Trump and many other recent presidents.

Primaries

The first primary took place in 1912 in North Dakota.[18] Now, most states hold primaries. Primaries are a patch on a bad system. They have made matters worse rather than better. They tend to favor the most extreme players in each party, and they are just another conflict that can get dirty and increase divisiveness. Negative ads and intense debates make enemies within parties.

Look at what it did to John McCann and Donald Trump. Even Kamala Harris and Joseph Biden had to do some "fence mending" after the Democratic primaries in 2020. The current system unavoidably damages personal relationships.

Vote Counting

The vote-counting method we have used for two hundred years is not the only way to measure voter support for candidates. At least two other methods are in use elsewhere, and both appear to have advantages over the prevailing system. One method is called rank-choice voting and can be done over the Internet.[19] Newer processes exist. Other countries use methods worthy of examination. We need to investigate our options. But piecemeal changes to a process for counting voter support should not be made without examining the entire election system. Processes link people and technology in every system. A change in one element of a system might necessitate other changes. Patches often fail to produce better outcomes.

"Two basic rules of life are: 1) Change is inevitable.
2) Everybody resists change."[20]

–W. Edwards Deming

This entire chapter has been about change. It lists major changes that have occurred and outlines how they have changed our lives, almost always for the better in the long run. One of Deming's most important ideas has to do with change itself. Rather than allow our natural resistance to change to impede our progress, we must welcome change and constantly seek out changes that lead to improvement. We Americans pride ourselves on the fact that we have not needed to make many changes to our Constitution. Perhaps it is time to rethink that logic.

The Constitution establishes our system of governance. Like every other system, it needs to be changed and improved upon using new ideas and advances in technology. It needs to be adapted to current circumstances. Changes have occurred, but we are due for more, as evidenced by recent events. This concept applies equally to the topic of emphasis in this book: our election system.

When you hear a politician talking about a position on an issue such as immigration, don't automatically accept that position. It could be the same old position that his party has always taken. Ask yourself whether the position takes into account all that has changed or is it more rhetoric designed to stir up emotions. Problem solving relies on gaining a deep understanding of the current situation. Logical thinking is required, and high emotions don't contribute to clear thinking.

In Chapter 4, we will look at some politicians who were masters of productivity. They were also masters at recognizing a need for change and making change happen. We can learn a great deal from the example they set.

Selected Quotes

"Each system is perfectly designed to give you exactly what you are getting today."

"Manage the cause, not the result."

"Management by results is like driving a car
looking in the rearview mirror."

"The big problems are where people don't
realize they have one in the first place."

"In God we trust; all others bring data."

"Eighty-five percent of the reasons for failure are deficiencies
in the system and process rather than the employee. The
role of management is to change the process rather than
badgering individuals to do better."

–W. Edwards Deming[20]

"Don't fight the problem, decide it."

"Go right straight down the road, to do what is best,
and do it frankly and without evasion."

"Democracy is the most demanding of all forms of
government in terms of the energy, imagination,
and public spirit required of the individual."

"What other people do shouldn't affect you—we do things
because of the kind of person we each want to be."

"The only way human beings can win a war is to prevent it."

–George C. Marshall[21]

Class of 1962 Graduation Speaker
June 6, 1962, West Point, President Kennedy's Arrival.
Author front row, far right.

Chapter 4

Masters of Productivity

P roductivity, getting the right things done in the best way possible, and wealth are related. We use Gross Domestic Product to reflect both productivity and wealth. The more productive an entity is, the more wealth it can distribute, which in part explains the vast wealth of individuals such as Bill Gates, one of the founders of Microsoft; Jeff Bezos, the founder of Amazon; and the late Steve Jobs, a founder of Apple. The same logic explains the wealth of America. We are productive people.

Some of our presidents have been extraordinarily productive, contributing to a better lifestyle for Americans. We are going to take a close look at some of their individual achievements. In all probability, none of the presidents in this chapter were disciples of Dr. Deming. They were natural-born problem solvers. They were consensus builders. They were leaders who chose to serve. They are the type of politicians we need.

Deming didn't create a new system for solving problems. He articulated a system and refined it with modern concepts and technology. He placed emphasis on the need to work as a team rather than as opponents. He did not believe in permanent solutions. After solving a problem, the team needs to celebrate and then start working on further improvement. His approach relies heavily on the collection of data to look for problems and to evaluate the effectiveness of solutions put in place. It is a methodical, pragmatic technique that sees undesirable results as a reflection of a process or system-wide failure. Rarely are the people or technology at fault, and when they are, the fix is simple.

I looked at many groups that ranked presidential performance. There were some major differences in the rankings beyond the top ten, but there was almost total agreement on those in the top ten spots and even more on the top five. I relied mostly on the C-SPAN rankings done in 2017.[2]

George Washington

Perhaps one of the most interesting things about George Washington is that he didn't want to be president. He was a plantation owner and had served his fledgling country for many years in hardship throughout the Revolutionary War. He had also been in military service for many years before that time. He wanted to return to his farm and home in Northern Virginia. When he won the election, the capital was New York City. In 1789, Philadelphia became the capital city and would remain so until May 1800[3]; consequently, he would again be taken from the Mount Vernon home he loved. What later became Washington, D.C. was picked to be the new capital in July 1790 because it was near the geographic center of the thirteen states. The location was important because of the slow modes of transportation at that time. It took ten years to get the new city ready. President Washington spent his eight years as president in Philadelphia.

President Washington did not have to do anything to get elected. He unsuccessfully resisted the pressure to take office. His eight years as president were the capstone of a lifetime of service. In the current election system, I doubt we could find people like Washington whom we could convince to run for president. If we changed the system, however, we would choose only people of competence and character who feel that serving the nation unselfishly is their duty.

President Washington is ranked so high because he set the highest possible standards of conduct for the future holders of that office. He established many traditions that have served us well. He started the tradition of remaining in office only two terms, and he participated in a smooth transition of power. He led us to victory in the war and led the way for a new democracy to carry out its responsibilities under a new system spelled out in the Constitution.

Washington also demonstrated his prowess as a problem solver by defeating the British and perceiving problems that were headed our way and are now causing us major difficulty. He warned us about political parties and said to be careful whom we place in power.

At the end of this chapter, I have included some quotes from George Washington and others that I mention. I try to incorporate some of the best and most appropriate quotes into the body of the chapter, knowing that a chuckle here and there is always welcome, so here are a few from Washington:[4]

"A pack of jackasses led by a lion is superior to a pack of lions led by a jackass."

"Occupants of public office love power
and are prone to abuse it."

"However [political parties] may now and then answer
popular ends, they are likely in the course of time and things
to become potent engines, by which cunning, ambitious,
and unprincipled men will be enabled to subvert the power
of the people and to usurp for themselves the reins of
government, destroying afterwards the very engines which
have lifted them to unjust dominion."

It is doubtful that anyone other than George Washington could have started America on a better path. He was a dedicated servant who had extraordinary skills and integrity. Those attributes earned him the respect and confidence of our founding fathers and the citizens of America.

Abraham Lincoln

Unlike George Washington, Abraham Lincoln was not well known or highly respected when he ran for president. If anything, he was denigrated because of his rural roots and appearance. He was from Illinois, the far western part of the establishment. He was sometimes referred to as the "original gorilla."[5] He had little or no formal education and lacked what easterners saw as refinement, and even his reputation for honesty was a matter for scorn, especially among politicians. He didn't like to be called Abe because sometimes people substituted a "p" for the "b," producing "Ape." He was not popular with voters during his first presidential campaign. He was elected with only about 40% of the popular vote but won the electoral vote by a landslide.[6] By only a slim margin, he carried the northern states, where the bulk of the electoral votes came from. He lost the southern states by big numbers. He took office when the country was divided over slavery and states' rights. Within thirty-nine days of his inauguration in 1861, the country was in a civil war.

President Lincoln took a unique approach to staffing his cabinet. He filled the key positions with his rivals for the presidency. He went on to win the respect, confidence, and even personal affection of all but one of those men. Cabinet members soon realized that he was many times smarter than he looked and that they had grossly underestimated him.[7]

Lincoln named William Seward Secretary of State. Seward had been one of Lincoln's fiercest rivals but later became his strongest supporter and a close friend. Seward was chided for "Seward's Folly," when, in March 1867, he made the "stupid mistake" of buying Alaska from Russia at a cost of about two cents an acre.

Lincoln built a team of strong, dedicated public servants. Together, they took on the task of preserving the Union. He and his team were successful.

Lincoln had many setbacks, especially in finding the right man to lead the Union Army, but eventually, he put Ulysses S. Grant in command after he repeatedly demonstrated his competence in the field. One story about Lincoln and Grant illustrates Lincoln's pragmatic and laser-like focus on his mission. One of Lincoln's staff members reported that there were rumors that General Grant was a heavy drinker. Lincoln suggested he find out what kind of whiskey Grant was fond of and send a case to all of the other Union Army generals.[8]

President Lincoln won the war and won reelection. He beat George B. McClellan, whom Lincoln had dismissed as the Union Army commander. The electoral vote count in 1864 was 212 to 12, and Lincoln had more than 55% of the popular vote.[9]

The war was in the final stages when voters went to the polls. Many people questioned whether the election should be held.

President Lincoln believed it essential that there be an election. His second inauguration was on March 4, 1865. He was assassinated forty-one days later by John Wilkes Booth, a Confederate sympathizer and a member of a disgruntled group of southerners.

Abraham Lincoln holds one of the top two spots in the ranking of all U.S. presidents because he was a man of extraordinary competence and character, as was George Washington. He achieved his objective to keep the Union together because of his focus and determination. His vice president was Andrew Johnson, who is ranked as one of our worst presidents. How different would the United States be today if John Wilkes Booth had not shot Lincoln to death in 1865? Below is a fitting quote often attributed to Lincoln:

"Nations do not die from invasion;
they die from internal rottenness." [10]

Franklin D. Roosevelt

Of the presidents covered in this chapter, Franklin D. Roosevelt (FDR) might have used the techniques of TQM better than any other. FDR was elected president in 1932. He ran against the incumbent Herbert Hoover, who was making little headway dealing with the Great Depression, which started with the stock market crash of 1929. FDR's campaign slogan was "Happy days are here again."[11] He was quite the optimist. He was the first and only president to serve more than two terms. He remained president for more than twelve years and led America through much of the Depression and most of World War II.

He did many things exceptionally well. He created complicated systems to accomplish gigantic tasks, including winning a worldwide war and providing economic relief to Americans in ways never done before. He saw problems coming and helped prepare the country to meet those problems, even though he had to fight resistance from influential Americans such as Joseph Kennedy, our ambassador to Great Britain, and Charles Lindberg, the aviation pioneer.[12]

Upon being introduced to a potential technological development that could determine the winner of the war, FDR took full advantage of the opportunity. He used relatively new technology, radio, to make more than thirty radio broadcasts, called "Fireside Chats," to keep Americans informed.[13] He was masterful at strategizing and prioritizing.

FDR put the right people in the right jobs. His wife, Eleanor, was his ambassador. She traveled the country and spoke to the electorate as would any politician and brought her impressions back to FDR.[14]

Here are two of FDR's quotes that show how his thinking mirrored that of Deming:[15]

"People acting together or as a group can accomplish things which no individual acting alone could ever hope to bring about."

"Do something. If it works, do more of it.
If it doesn't, do something else."

FDR was disabled. He had polio when he was a young man. In 1921, he could barely stand up and needed aid to walk. He spent most of his time in a wheelchair. Regardless of his physical disability, he served in many important positions in government before becoming president.

Upon taking office in 1933, he started implementing the New

Deal, the start of Social Security, and many other programs to lift the country out of the Depression. One program was the Civilian Conservation Corps (CCC). My own father worked on CCC projects in our national parks, constructing infrastructure that generations of Americans have enjoyed.

World War I was not out of mind yet, but by the late 1930s, the prospect of another major war was building. The last thing Americans wanted to hear about was another war with Germany. FDR believed it was likely, however, and had to prepare the country. He started a program called Lend/Lease. Although not well received at the time, it accomplished two important objectives. It increased the capability of future American allies by sending much-needed war supplies to Russia and Great Britain and helped them resist the aggression of the Axis powers. Second, it expanded production facilities we would need to fight a war. We were still unprepared for a major war when the Japanese attacked Pearl Harbor on December 7, 1941, but Lend/Lease and other steps FDR had taken helped us.

In August 1939, FDR received a letter from Albert Einstein.[16] It advised FDR that new technology ($E=mc^2$) might make it possible to produce a new weapon with the potential to cause destruction of such magnitude that whoever mastered the technology first would win the war. Einstein thought it possible that German scientists were already at work on such a weapon. Einstein sent two more letters, the last in April 1940.[17]

By 1942, the Manhattan Project, its mission to produce an atomic bomb, was up and running. Dr. Julius Oppenheimer was the lead physicist, and General Leslie R. Groves was the project manager.[18] Groves had been the project manager for the construction of the Pentagon,[19] then and still the largest office building in the world. The Manhattan Project was treated as a super-secret undertaking. Vice President Harry Truman did not learn of the project until FDR died in April 1945.

FDR put together a team of generals to fight the war and a team of civilians to create the industrial capabilities needed to produce the materials required for a war like no other in history. General George C. Marshall led the military team. General Douglas MacArthur was his commander for all forces in the Pacific Theater. General Dwight Eisenhower was the commander of all Allied forces in Europe. FDR established the War Production Board. Members included chief executive officers of major corporations such as Campbell Soup and General Electric.[20] One member was a leader of the American Federation of Labor. In 1940, the United States produced 6,000 military aircraft. In 1943, it made 85,000.[21]

There is a saying that "An army moves on its stomach." Yes, you need well trained, well armed, and well led troops to fight a war. You also need ships, airplanes, tanks, cannons, food, medical supplies, and much more. We were not prepared for war, and FDR knew it. He had to buy time until the country could build the machine it would need to go on the offensive. America had few early successes on the battlefield. FDR was convinced that the United States could not win if it split its efforts between Europe and Asia. He had to prioritize. FDR focused on beating the Axis powers in Europe before going after Japan. MacArthur was ordered to evacuate the Philippines and allow the Japanese to take control. MacArthur disagreed and almost chose not to obey. At the last moment, he evacuated to Australia, where he remained in a defensive role for years. When it was clear that the war in Europe was almost over, MacArthur was given permission to go on the offensive. FDR's strategy worked.

FDR did exactly as Dr. Deming said we should when taking on a project (such as becoming president in 1933). Roosevelt saw the problems already in place or headed his way and took them on with teams of capable people. He defined the problems and set clear objectives. He used people and technology, even technology that was unproven. He was a great strategic thinker. He brought the country out of the Depression and ensured that it emerged from war as a military and economic power. This is why he is one of the top ten American presidents.

Thomas Jefferson

Thomas Jefferson was one of our most visible founding fathers. He was a Virginian, as was George Washington, but Washington was a soldier, while Jefferson was a statesman and intellectual. One of Jefferson's most notable acts was to author the Declaration of Independence. When President John F. Kennedy was hosting a reception for a group of Nobel Prize winners, he remarked, "I think this is the most extraordinary collection of talent, of human knowledge, that has ever gathered together at the White House, with the possible exception of when Thomas Jefferson dined alone."[22]

Our third president, Jefferson was in office from 1801 to 1809. He pushed our westward expansion by making the Louisiana Purchase. He had the foresight to send Lewis and Clark on a mission to explore the West. An advocate of education, he played a role in founding the U.S. Military Academy at West Point in 1802. After his time as president, he founded the University of Virginia in 1817.[23] He loved to read and put great value on books.

Jefferson also might have had skills in magic. He reduced taxes and drastically cut the national debt,[24] even after completing the Louisiana Purchase. We desperately need more presidents who have mastered that trick.

Jefferson was a thinker and a doer. He didn't have to take on major problems such as wars or a depression, but he didn't coast. He made improvements that extended our country far to the west and made it possible for us eventually to occupy all of the land from the Atlantic Ocean to the Pacific.

Honorable Mention

Many more presidents deserve special recognition for one reason or another, but I will list only three more. I've picked those who demonstrated a principle of TQM, accomplished an especially impressive task, or gave us a memorable quote.

Theodore Roosevelt is in the top ten on most ranking lists. He is known for his service in the Spanish/American War and for being the force behind the Panama Canal. France had undertaken the task of building the canal and failed. Teddy Roosevelt took up the challenge and got it done. The key was getting the right person and the right technology involved. Roosevelt brought in an engineer, John Stevens, who saw the problem differently from his predecessors.[25] The problem was not digging; it was moving the dirt. He had a train system built. Hauling the rubble away with railroad cars was a major improvement. One of Roosevelt's quotes should also be in the top ten:

"When they call the roll in the Senate, the senators do not know whether to answer 'Present' or 'Not Guilty.'" [26]

When I was eight, I was the proud wearer of an "I like Ike" button. Dwight Eisenhower was a military superstar. Just before World War II, he was a lowly lieutenant colonel. At the end of the war, he was a five-star general and commander of all Allied Forces in Europe.[27] He held the highest rank attainable. He was not considered a military genius, as was General MacArthur, who also wore five stars. Instead, Eisenhower was considered a master at building cohesion among military and political leaders. He used the same skill as president. He was a team leader. He was not ashamed to borrow good ideas from others. One of his legacies is our federal interstate highway system. He saw the federally controlled highway system in Germany, the autobahn, and created a similar system in the United States. His quotes are more on the profound side than the humorous, but this one is both:

"The middle of the road is all the usable surface. The extremes, right and left, are in the gutter." [28]

Harry Truman became president when FDR died in 1945. He made the difficult decision to use atomic bombs on Japan. He looked at the projections as to the number of American lives that would be lost if we had to invade Japan as we did Europe. He warned the Japanese people that we were going to unleash a weapon of unimaginable power if they did not surrender. They refused. Truman dropped the first bomb on Hiroshima. They still did not surrender, so he dropped the second bomb three days later on Nagasaki. The larger bomb had the explosive equivalent of 40,000,000 pounds of TNT.[29] The bombs killed somewhere between 129,000 and 226,000 people.[30]

Within five years, we were again at war in the Far East, this time against North Korea and later China. We ran the war from Japan. President Truman did not have an easy time in office, but he maintained his sense of humor:

"My choice early in life was to be a piano player in a whorehouse or a politician. To tell the truth, there's hardly a difference." [31]

All seven of these presidents were capable and dedicated public servants. Two of the top three died in office. FDR survived an assassination attempt in 1933[32] and served until he died of a massive cerebral hemorrhage in 1945. He was sixty-three and just starting his fourth term in office. Abraham Lincoln was starting his second term when he was assassinated in 1865. He had just turned fifty-four. George Washington endured the freezing cold winters of the North while fighting the British, and maybe even worse, he coped with limited public support for the war that often left his soldiers unpaid and without the clothing and food they desperately needed. All seven presidents surrounded themselves with the best people they could find and put them in the right jobs. Lincoln made Ulysses Grant commander of the Union Army. Teddy Roosevelt put John Stevens in charge of building the Panama Canal. FDR didn't make the mistake of putting a "thinker" (Einstein) in charge of the Manhattan Project. He put a proven "doer," Leslie R. Groves, in charge. Thomas Jefferson sent Lewis and Clark to explore the West. Dwight Eisenhower was the epitome of a team leader. And Harry Truman made the decision to drop two atomic bombs on Japan rather than endure a long and deadly invasion.

You might disagree with some of the actions these men took. That is understandable. I mentioned them because they were supremely productive, in many cases under circumstances that were horrific, and got big things done using techniques that reflect the ideas W. Edwards Deming put forth as part of TQM. These men played major roles in shaping, building, and protecting the United States of America.

Use these presidents as reference models when you are evaluating candidates and their ideals. America and Americans thrive on productivity. These seven leaders delivered. Is the candidate or party you are listening to pushing for productivity or for stopping the productivity of the opposition? If they are pushing for the latter, think about whether we can continue to have a political environment where it is impossible to get things done. Remember, too, that if any special-interest group can stymie change, changes that the majority want, the system of democracy is not performing to its potential.

Selected Quotes

These quotes are sometimes funny and almost always include ideas connected to TQM. If you look for more quotes from the same people, you might find some that are offensive but a reflection of their times. Some might have been said in an attempt to sway a particular audience, although that excuse isn't great, either. Like all human beings, these men were not perfect. They did much more good than bad, however. Pay attention to the problems these men were alluding to in these quotes and the time that has elapsed. We should all be concerned that so little progress has been made in solving problems that go so far back.

"Be Americans. Let there be no sectionalism,
no North, South, East, or West. You are all
dependent on one another and should be one union.
Be Americans, and be true to yourselves."

"Occupants of public office love power
and are prone to abuse it."

"When one side of a story is heard and often repeated, the
human mind becomes impressed with it insensibly."

"What is most important of this grand experiment, the
United States? Not the election of the first president but

the election of the second. The peaceful transition of
power is what will separate this country from
every other country in the world."

"Truth will ultimately prevail where there is pain
taken to bring it to light."

–George Washington[4]

"If our public ever dies, it will be from suicide,
from degeneracy."[33]

"Nearly all men can stand adversity, but if you want to test a
man's character, give him power."[34]

"I laugh because I must not cry, that is all, that is all."[34]

"I am a firm believer in the people. If given the truth, they can
be depended upon to meet any national crisis. The great
point is to bring them the facts."[34]

"Do I not destroy my enemies when I
make them my friends?"[34]

–Abraham Lincoln

"Repetition does not transform a lie into a truth."[15]

"Never underestimate a man who overestimates himself."[15]

"We must especially beware of that small group of selfish
men who would clip the wings of the American eagle in
order to feather their own nests."[15]

"Democracy cannot succeed unless those expressing their choice are prepared to choose wisely. The real safeguard of democracy, therefore, is education."[35]

–Franklin D. Roosevelt

"When the people are afraid of the government, that's tyranny. But when the government is afraid of the people, that's liberty."

"When you abandon freedom to achieve security, you lose both and deserve neither."

"The government you elect is the government you deserve."

–Thomas Jefferson[36]

"Knowing what is right doesn't mean much unless you do what's right."

"All contributions by corporations to any political committee or for any political purpose should be forbidden by law."

"The most important single ingredient in the formula for success is knowing how to get along with people."

"This country will not be a good place for any of us to live in unless we make it a good place for all of us to live in."

–Theodore Roosevelt[26]

"The supreme quality of leadership is integrity."

"A people that values its privileges above
its principles soon loses both."

"Every step we take toward making the State our caretakers
of our lives, by that much we move toward making
the State our master."

–Dwight Eisenhower[1]

"It is amazing what you can accomplish if you do not care
who gets the credit."[31]

"Without a strong educational system—free of government
control—democracy is crippled. Knowledge is not only the
key to power; it is the citadel of human freedom."[31]

"I never did give anyone hell. I just told the truth and they
thought it was hell."[31]

"Term limits would cure both senility and seniority, both
terrible legislative diseases."[37]

–Harry Truman

Chapter 5

Total Quality Management (TQM)

"The aim proposed here for any organization is for everybody to gain—stockholders, employees, suppliers, customers, community, the government—over the long term." [1]

–W. Edwards Deming

M artin Spinner was in his plush office waiting for a potential new client to arrive for a ten o'clock meeting. Martin was a lawyer, a high-priced one, and he felt it necessary to show how successful he was by surrounding himself with the best of everything. Even his mechanical pencil was flamboyant, an antique Montblanc that enhanced his image. His prospective client arrived and must have been impressed because he agreed to use the lawyer's overpriced services. The next day, a Saturday, Martin took his oldest son out to play miniature golf. He paid for the round and picked up putters, a scorecard, two balls, and a stubby little wooden pencil.

In this hypothetical situation, let's add another event. Martin is back home and decides to do some work around the house. He needs to replace a long board on his deck. He has the board but it is too wide, so he needs to cut an inch off the full length of the board. He has a straight edge to mark the cut line, but what pencil should he use? He still has the cheap pencil from the mini-golf course, but the lead breaks on the rough surface of the board. The Montblanc performs no better. He goes to his workshop and finds a fat-leaded pencil he'd bought at a home improvement store. It does the job just fine.

In TQM, quality is not about cost, workmanship, aesthetics, or availability. Quality is all about *suitability*. All three pencils—the expensive Montblanc, the cheap stubby one from the golf course, and the fat-leaded pencil—are quality writing instruments designed and manufactured to meet the specialized needs of specific situations. All come to the marketplace and eventually the customer through productive systems comprised of people, technology, and process. These systems are created using backward design. The designers don't pay much attention to what is in place now. They start with the objective they desire. Once the systems are in place, they rely on feedback from customers and data-based analysis, wherever possible, to measure performance and make improvements. The success of these pencils is ultimately determined by the volume of sales at a price point that enables the owners of the systems to realize their goals.

TQM is central to this book. It is a great way to deal with problems and get things done that need to be done. I have repeated the message several times and in several different ways: if things are not getting done, changes have to be made. TQM is a way to change the way everything is done. The principles are applicable to every aspect of life. Politics and governance are not exceptions.

Many readers are familiar with the term "Quality Control." Without some training in TQM, it is easy to assume that these terms are similar, but they are distinct in an important way. Quality control is one aspect of TQM, but we will spend our time on the broader principles that form the foundation of TQM. The notion of quality control is best left to statisticians and mathematicians. My omission of that concept will facilitate rather than harm our discussion about TQM.

The successful implementation of TQM requires a complete change in how we think about people in general and how the various components of any organization interact. As outlined in Deming's quote at the start of this chapter, TQM focuses on a win-win outcome for all of the people in an organization.

According to Douglas McGregor in his 1960 book, *The Human Side of Enterprise*, there are two vastly different ways to view people, particularly employees. McGregor called them "Theory X" and "Theory Y."[2] McGregor's theories relative to the management of people are right up there with Einstein's theory of relativity in the field of physics.

Theory X

A typical worker has little ambition, avoids responsibility, and is individual-goal oriented. X-type managers believe their employees are less intelligent, lazy, and work solely for a sustainable income.

Theory Y

Employees are internally motivated, enjoy the job, and work to better themselves without a direct reward in return. Managers view their employees as valuable assets, and employees do not require close supervision to meet objectives. They require support.

At about the same time McGregor was expressing his ideas, a psychologist named Abraham Maslow presented what became known as "Maslow's Hierarchy of Needs." According to Maslow, humans are motivated by needs and always aspire for the next need that they don't have until they reach the highest need: self-actualization. It is something like being the best you can be and/or being true to yourself.[3] Maslow incorporated his theory with McGregor's and came up with Theory Z.[2] Maslow's Hierarchy of Needs appears at the end of this chapter.

Theory Z

An optimal managerial style cultivates workers' creativity, insight, meaning, and moral excellence.

Both McGregor and Maslow steered management toward a middle position. X and Y are not extremes on a single continuum. They are separate continua with their own extremes. Managers need to determine which style best suits their situation and where they should position themselves on that continuum. In general, the Theory X continuum is better suited for assembly lines and manual labor. The Theory Y continuum is for those who need more flexibility to perform their assigned tasks. The best results generally come from being more toward the middle on either continuum.[2]

Former Secretary of Commerce Malcolm Baldrige was a strong advocate of TQM. A national award is named for him and given each year to U.S. companies that demonstrate excellence in TQM. Below are remarks made by two former presidents during the presentations of the Malcolm Baldrige Award:

"America's economic strength depends on industry's ability to improve productivity and quality and to remain on the cutting edge of technology."[4]

–Ronald Reagan

When President Clinton gave the awards, he emphasized three things: customer satisfaction, workforce empowerment, and increased productivity.[5] TQM is a system for getting things done that incorporates modern ideas about human behavior. It requires a change in the way interrelated elements accomplish a common goal and how they treat each other. In TQM, this idea is called a "cultural change." Part of that change is to stop resisting change and embrace new ways to get things done.

Deming listed six components of an organization, and there might be even more, but I will talk about the three primary components in a profit-oriented business venture: owners/managers, employees, and customers. These groups are not mutually exclusive, but we will start out by treating them as three separate entities. I will refer to owners/managers as the "company."

Although all three components—company, employees and customers—need each other, they have traditionally interacted as if they were at odds rather than joined in a cooperative effort. From this point of view, each entity assumes that the way it can maximize what it derives from the relationship is to take care of itself first. If doing so causes harm to the other two participants, too bad but so be it. The company tries to get as much work as possible from employees at the lowest possible cost. The company tries to sell its product or service to customers at the highest price it can get, regardless of the result for customers. Employees resist new technology that helps the company because they believe this protects their jobs and they push the company to its limits to get the most pay and benefits. Most employees have little or no concern for customers. Many employees see no need to worry about the customer; the customer is invisible. The customer is also out to maximize his own interests. He sees no need to worry about employees; they are the company's problem. He uses the low-bid-wins system to get the most for the least, or he has the Purchasing Department do the hard negotiating so it can make the company yield. These preliminary contests set the stage for a strained long-term relationship between the company and the customer, one that frequently ends in mutual dissatisfaction.

I am generalizing and simplifying these interactions to compare more easily the two extremes of the traditional business model, as outlined above, and the TQM business model, which I will outline in a moment. First, here is a brief story.

I was visiting West Point in 2017 after having been away for many years. I was in a car with guys I had been in school with, and one of them was the head of all construction for the Air Force prior to his retirement. I said I was disappointed at the shoddy way the facilities looked. His response was, "You have to take into consideration that all the work done on base is awarded through the low-bid-wins system." A better term for it might be the "low-bid-low-performance" system.

In the TQM business model, all three entities still have the same objective: to get the most out of the relationship they can. However, they go about it in a different way. Rather than a culture of conflict, they strive for a culture of teamwork and mutual respect. They turn the traditional model completely around. Each entity believes and acts as if its best interests are served when it takes care of the other two entities in the relationship. The company takes care of employees and customers; the employees take care of the company and the customer; and the customer takes care of the company and company's employees. This shift is substantial, but the approach works in the right culture.

I will further highlight this difference in culture using a situation that all adults face. Quite frequently, we need to use a contractor to do something around our home or to repair our car. Customers have learned the hard way that many contractors over promise and under deliver. A "quality" contractor will do the reverse. This contractor will under promise and over deliver.

The mother of a high school student needs a home tutor to help her child with science. She gets the name of a tutor from a friend who is happy with the tutor she uses for her child. The mother and the tutor talk and agree that the tutor will work with her child every Wednesday from 3:00 in the afternoon to 4:00 for $70. The tutor intentionally arrives at 2:45 and starts the lesson as soon as the student is ready. The tutor does not stop the session until 4:15. This plan was in place from the beginning. The tutor is in demand because he exceeds expectations. If the mother wants to reciprocate in TQM fashion, she will give the tutor a tip, have cookies for him on his next visit, tell him how pleased she is with his services, and recommend him to others. It is the start of a win-win relationship.

I learned about and experienced TQM while I worked in management for P&G. Because of my security experience in the Army, however, I felt that my future was in security, and security was not in the mainstream of what P&G did. I eventually left and went to work for Allied Security. We provided uniformed security personnel to all types of organizations. In a senior management position with Allied, I was invited to enter into discussions with management at a large P&G paper plant that had many security officers. It was not a low-bid-wins situation, as was common in our industry. Allied folks talked at length with P&G about its expectations and presented the plant with a proposal for managing the project.

Our proposal included innovative concepts for paying our employees and a cost-plus pricing formula that I first encountered when I worked for P&G. It was the first time Allied used this technique. The P&G folks liked what we proposed but were concerned about our insistence that we have a manager on site. The Purchasing Department had to justify its existence, so it questioned the need for a manager because P&G would have to pay that expense. We made it clear that the on-site manager was essential to give P&G the service it expected. P&G asked us to try it without the manager. We compromised. We would try it with the on-site manager, and if it proved unnecessary, we would eliminate that position and the cost. All agreed. There would be a trial period.

When I retired about fifteen years later, Allied still had the service at that site as well as several other P&G locations. We still had a manager on site, and the contract was never put out for bid. Each year at contract renewal time, we met and discussed the wage and benefits changes we wanted to make and any other changes one or the other party felt appropriate. It was the TQM model at work. Allied, as the company (supplier), took care of our customer (P&G) and our employees. P&G made it possible for us to take good care of our employees and compensated us fairly. As a result, our employees were loyal to both Allied and P&G.

As with every interaction involving people, there were disagreements, as there should be, but the culture cultivated acceptable resolutions because of the mutual respect of the parties. All were members of a team with a shared goal. The members might disagree on the best way to do something, but in the end, they reached a compromise and moved forward as a cohesive unit.

To demonstrate the TQM culture more clearly, I will mention two things, one small and one large.

In our industry, taking customers to lunch was an expectation. The customer frequently selected an upscale restaurant and enjoyed a nice steak for lunch and one or two adult beverages. No one ever doubted who would pay the bill. Our contacts at P&G locations would not allow us to take them to lunch. At lunchtime, we would go to the company cafeteria, and each person would pay for his own meal. This small arrangement is indicative of a different way to interact, a different culture.

Here is the big thing. One of our Allied branch managers got in serious financial trouble and resorted to embezzlement. He over-billed customers and manipulated transfers to his account. The victims were our three largest customers in that city. The security directors knew each other because they were members of the local chapter of the American Society for Industrial Security. I was the vice president of operations, so the three security directors initiated a conference call with me. One of the directors was with P&G. He remained silent for most of the call. The other two took turns venting their anger and frustration. I heard repeatedly, "How could something like this happen?" "What are you going to do about this?" and "I assume you know we'll cancel the contract." A few minutes after the conference call ended, I received a call from the security manager at P&G. He apologized and assured me that he had full confidence in us and knew we would perform a thorough investigation and solve the problem to his supervisors' satisfaction. We kept the P&G contract, and we lost the other two.

When I was in the security department at P&G, we investigated numerous incidents of employee embezzlement and theft. I'd bet the two security managers at those two other firms had done the same thing. What made them think we were immune to the same type of behavior that every major organization experiences? I never asked them that question because in TQM, the customer is always right, but some customers are a lot more right than others.

It's time for further discussion about human behavior. But first, here's Aesop's fable "The Scorpion and the Frog":[6]

A scorpion and a frog meet on the bank of a stream. The scorpion can't swim, so it asks the frog to carry him across on its back. The frog asks, "How do I know you won't sting me?" The scorpion says, "Because if I do, I will die too." The frog is satisfied, and they set out, but midstream, the scorpion stings the frog. The frog feels the onset of paralysis and starts to sink, knowing they both will drown, but has just enough time to gasp, "Why?" The scorpion replies, "Because it's my nature."

In one version, the scorpion waits until they are almost on the shore and then stings the frog so that only the frog dies. The moral in the first version is that people, like the scorpion, rarely can change their basic nature, even if it costs them their own lives. In the second version, the scorpion uses deceitfulness and cleverness to get across the stream, but he still kills the frog because it is his nature to kill, even when he should be thankful to the frog.

This is the perfect place for another great Einstein quote: "If you want your children to be intelligent, read them fairy tales. If you want them to be more intelligent, read them more fairy tales."[7]

Every aspect of human behavior can be placed on a continuum, and there are hundreds if not thousands of continua. No two people are alike. Almost all of us will read an article in the paper or see a story on TV and wonder why someone would run into a burning building to rescue a handicapped person, give a kidney to an unknown person, or enter a mall and shoot six people. For the most part, it is their nature. Just as Maslow states in his hierarchy of needs, all human beings, given the opportunity, want to self-actualize. Fortunately, or unfortunately in some cases, what makes us be true to ourselves is different from person to person. In a way, every person is greedy. People want to be fulfilled. The big question is what it takes for them to feel fulfilled. To place people in a system and get a particular task accomplished, you have to be able to define the nature of the people who are best suited to perform that task in accordance with your expectations. That quality in TQM is called "suitability."

Many tools are available to measure specific aspects of a person's nature and compare that person on a scale with those of the general population. The tools I cover below were used to evaluate me when I was working, and I used these tools to evaluate people when I was doing the hiring. My purpose is to demonstrate how many variables there are in human behavior and how they can be applied to forecast future performance. I will also touch on the science behind some of the tools because it reveals a great deal about human behavior and how psychologists use their knowledge of people to get meaningful data.

Houghton Mifflin publishes a test called "A Study of Values." The questionnaire takes less than thirty minutes to complete. Evaluation is easy. Anyone with minimal training can evaluate it. The outcome compares the individual's values with those of the general population in six areas:

Power: needs to influence and control others

Financial: wants money and property

Theoretical: strives for knowledge and understanding

Social: wants to be of service to others,
            particularly those less fortunate

Aesthetic: seeks beauty and harmony with nature

Religious: finds comfort in a spiritual lifestyle

The test-taker must make choices, and the outcome must be a balance among the values. No one can be above the 50% ranking in all six areas. A representative outcome would be something like the following:

Power:	80%
Financial:	65%
Theoretical:	70%
Social:	20%
Aesthetic:	30%
Religious:	35%

Note that using 50% as the midpoint, the three values over 50% are higher by a total of sixty-five percentage points, and the three values below 50% are lower by a total of sixty-five percentage points, representing the balance I was referring to.

Assume we were looking for a person to sell vacuum cleaners door to door. We would take a sampling of the top salespeople and have them complete the questionnaire. After compiling the results, our measurement of the best candidates' values might look this way:

Power:	90%
Financial:	95%
Theoretical:	60%
Social:	5%
Aesthetic:	10%
Religious:	40%

If we were looking for an art teacher in a rural community, the following might be our target:

Power:	25%	
Financial:	10%	
Theoretical:	70%	
Social:	75%	
Aesthetic:	90%	
Religious:	30%	

Now I am going to venture into unknown territory and try to envision the values of a bad politician and then a good politician. I have presented the figures side by side to make the comparison easier. Alone with each value are my thoughts:

	Good	Bad
Power:	60%	95%
Power causes conflict. Less conflict is desirable.		
Financial:	50%	80%
We want them to serve us, not themselves.		
Theoretical:	70%	30%
A drive to learn and do things is good.		
Social:	50%	30%
They need to care about others.		
Aesthetic:	25%	20%
No significant difference here.		
Religious:	45%	45%
No difference.		

The exact numbers are not important. What is important is that character matters, and we can measure certain character traits and match them with the traits of those who are doing the job the way we want it done.

Another method to measure and compare behavior is the DISC

system. Developed by psychologist William Moulton Marston,[8] the DISC assessment examines how an individual ranks in four areas of behavior and especially how the person interacts with others:

> **Dominance:** People of this personality type tend to be confident and place an emphasis on accomplishing bottom-line results. They tend to have active behavior in an unfriendly environment.
>
> **Influence:** People of this personality type tend to be more open and place an emphasis on relationships and influencing or persuading others. They tend to have active behavior in a friendly environment.
>
> **Steadiness:** People of this personality type tend to be dependable and place the emphasis on cooperation and sincerity. They tend to exhibit passive behavior in a friendly environment. At a party, they might be referred to as "wall flowers."
>
> **Consciousness:** People of this personality type tend to place the emphasis on quality, accuracy, expertise, and competency. They tend to have passive behavior in an unfriendly environment.

Again, there must be a balance between what is above the 50% line and what is below. Here are the ratings for the classical salesperson position:

Dominance:	75%
Influence:	90%
Steadiness:	10%
Consciousness:	25%

That profile reflects an active person who can handle an unfriendly environment and work hard to convert it into a friendly one, where he is most comfortable. He is impatient and will comply only reluctantly. He will be late turning in sales call logs and expense reports.

Below are the rankings for an entrepreneur:

Dominance: 99%
Influence: 70%
Steadiness: 30%
Consciousness: 1%

This profile indicates an extreme entrepreneur. People with this profile will go out of their way to create an unfriendly environment. They interrupt and belittle others. They love conflict and hate conformity. If people have the gall to speak out against a person with this profile, they become enemies forever. People with this profile are sore losers.

Most people who have been involved in hiring people do not need to use written questionnaires. They understand behavior and know how to define behavior by talking with people or viewing their past performance.

I want to mention another device, one that measures an individual's propensity to lie. I am not talking about a machine; it's a questionnaire. The psychology behind this questionnaire tells us a lot about human nature. Most people use themselves as a major part of their reference system when answering questions about moral conduct. Their second reference group is the people they associate with, and thieves generally associate with other thieves, especially if they end up in prison, and liars commonly hang out with others like themselves. So when asked a simple question such as "What was the largest amount of money you ever stole?" their thinking follows this kind of logic: "I once stole $5,000, so I can't admit to that, but everybody I know has stolen at least $3,000, so they'll know I am lying if I say $2,000, so I'll answer $2,800." This individual has performed just the way the psychologists expect.

People's character matters as does the character (culture) of a group when we are working to accomplish a goal. It makes no difference whether the group is a business, a sports team, a social community, or a government department.

Every group needs a clearly stated objective that represents the combined thinking of the group's members. In TQM, this objective takes the form of a mission statement. Writing a mission statement is hard for one person, much less a group of people with mixed needs and varying attitudes about where they want to go and how they want to get there. Without a mission statement, preparing a plan to reach a certain goal is impossible, as is knowing when the group has achieved it. In TQM, a mission statement comes out of a democratic effort.

Assume a family of two senior parents, their three middle-aged children, and six young-adult grandchildren, two per couple, all want to go on a vacation together. They have agreed that each of the four households will pay their own expenses. The first step in the process they have chosen is for each unit to come to agreement among themselves on what they want for a vacation and to select a spokesperson. The representatives from each unit then meet and strive to reach agreement on what the entire family will do for vacation. If they agree and go on a vacation together, they have done a great job. If they return from the vacation and all are still talking to one another, they have done a fantastic job and have probably had some TQM training!

Now imagine writing a mission statement for a panel put together to create a better election system or a better system of governance. You might think that achieving agreement on a better election method is almost impossible and that reaching a consensus on a mission statement dealing with governance *is* impossible. Unfortunately, we don't have the option of not trying. Without a destination, we will go aimlessly from one position to another, and, in all probability, we will be locked into a "doing-and-undoing" cycle. U.S. administrations have actually done both.

We tried to address election system problems with the Federal Election Campaign Act of 1971[9] and the creation of the Federal Election Commission (FEC) in 1974. Both were poor attempts and have been largely ineffective, but at least people saw a problem and tried to address it. The FEC came up with a mission statement, one that was narrow in scope: "The FEC is an independent regulatory agency . . . whose purpose is to enforce campaign finance laws. . . . The commission describes its duties as: disclose campaign finance information, enforce provisions of the law, and oversee the public funding of presidential elections."

As evidence of the ineffectiveness of the commission, it was unable to function from August 2019 to December 2020 because it lacked a quorum.[9] I am sure it is just a coincidence that this fifteen-month period coincided with the 2020 election and had nothing to do with the fact that the president appoints members and the Senate confirms those appointed. In golf, a disastrous shot receives a do-over called a mulligan. In other words, the best way to proceed after total failure is to start over.

We did much better with our mission statement for governance. In fact, we did it twice and had good success with both. The Declaration of Independence is basically a mission statement. It set forth our path for the period from July 4, 1776 until September 7, 1787, when our Constitution was signed by George Washington, who was president of the constitutional convention, and the other state deputies. The Declaration of Independence is still part of our mission statement, but the preamble to the

Constitution added the following: "We the People of the United States, in order to form a more perfect union, establish justice, insure domestic tranquility, provide for the common defense, promote the general welfare, and secure the blessings of liberty to ourselves and our posterity, do ordain and establish this Constitution for the United States of America."

The document itself, including the amendments, then goes on to establish the mechanics of governance.

Considering the age of both documents, their brevity, and the changes that have taken place since 1776, they have served us remarkably well. We can make improvements. We should never stop checking to ensure that our mission statement is consistent with our current and foreseeable aspirations and that we are using the best systems we can devise to achieve our mission. We need to take an in-depth look at our current position, as Thomas Jefferson did when he cited a long list of grievances with Britain, and decide where we want to go and how we can best get there. If it is agreed that our mission is the same as it was in 1787, we need to educate citizens so they know that mission and expect nothing more and nothing less. It is also okay if we choose to clarify or modernize the mission statement. In essence, we want consensus on what we are striving to be as a nation and how to move toward that objective. Unlike football, when we get close to the goal line, we should push our objective back further. In the terminology of TQM , this concept is called "continuous improvement." Some readers might have questions about TQM. The answers will be helpful.

Wasn't General Motors' Saturn car division a TQM-based company? If so, why did it fail?

It was most definitely TQM-designed from top to bottom, but design and execution are not the same thing. Some factors, such as timing, come into play and are beyond control. With Saturn, everything was new: the plant, employees, manufacturing system, product, dealers, hassle-free sales technique, and customer care. Some people think Saturn tried to do too much at one time.[10] The product—cars—were okay, but not special. Great cars would have been helpful when launching a new brand. Saturn's whole new way of selling cars was so strange that customers were skeptical. The sales technique might have been hassle-free, but people wondered whether they were paying full price when other dealers gave them a great deal by cutting the sticker price. To make matters worse, the recession in 1990 hurt all car sales. One of Deming's quotes also might apply: "American management thinks they can just copy from Japan. But they don't know what to copy."[11]

Isn't TQM just a variation of communism?

No. Both require a change in culture, but they are different in a subtle but significant respect. Individuals strive to achieve self-actualization, and highly productive people want the rewards that come from their productivity. What they do with those rewards is up to them. Communism requires a change in human nature. Under communism, the productive person must pass the wealth to those who are less productive. This obligation frequently leads to declining productivity, as in Cuba and Venezuela. TQM intends to achieve higher levels of productivity by using a culture built on teamwork and cooperation. The distribution changes only in that the amount to distribute increases. Communism is a distribution/re-distribution system that tends to decrease productivity and frequently results in authoritarian leadership, as it has in North Korea. TQM is a production system that has little to do with redistribution of wealth and is a democratic process that can thrive in a democracy.

What's the downside of TQM?

There are two. Just as participants in a democratic society have to be educated to understand the issues and make good choices as citizens, the workers in a TQM culture have to be knowledgeable so they can make meaningful contributions to a team effort. They have to be able to operate independently and to understand and accept the type of conduct expected of them. This adjustment might be difficult for some.

The second downside is more troublesome. TQM is a pragmatic approach for getting things done. People with idealistic goals, especially those who want to reach their goals without a plan that gives them a reasonable chance to succeed, will dislike TQM. In 1919, the Eighteenth Amendment, known as Prohibition, was passed. I doubt a plan was in place to make this amendment succeed. If so, it had to be one of the worst plans ever devised. Prohibition was an idealistic dream that became a nightmare. Although it was idealistic in nature, it failed because it was an unworkable system. Prohibition ended not because our ideals shifted. Yes, we did and undid prohibition over a fourteen-year period, but the doing and undoing we experience today is due to the shifting back and forth between the ideals of the left and those of the right. In TQM, or any other management system, it makes no difference how an objective comes to be. That objective will not reach fruition unless the majority of the people support it and a very pragmatic plan is in place to make it happen. Prohibition came undone because the goal was unfeasible. The wall on the border with Mexico will be undone because of a change in the party controlling the White House.

We have entered into "wars" on many vices—alcohol, drugs, gambling, and prostitution—and we haven't won any of them. These wars have too many Americans fighting for the opposition. In a perfect world, we might be able to outlaw these vices, but we live in a world that is far from perfect, and we have many other problems to manage. We had to surrender unconditionally in our war against the evils of alcohol. We are slowly retreating in our wars against drugs and gambling. As a pragmatist, I like the saying, "If you can't beat 'em, join 'em." Consider the tax revenue we have gained from alcohol and gambling.

Idealists will find many downsides to TQM. They will say we are abandoning the high road. They are right, but our reasoning is sound: no one has been able to show us the way to get there from here. According to McGregor, "An objective without a plan is a dream."[12]

In addition to the vices, we now face another divisive and challenging situation with the pragmatists on one side and the idealists on the other. The issue is immigration, and the border wall is part of the issue. This situation is different from the vices in that the "high road" is accessible if we can come to grips with relatively new complications. Immigration was much easier to manage before FDR's New Deal went into effect and before the threat of foreign terrorists reached the level it has now. We must first clearly define the immigration problem. Part of that definition calls for deciding which government-provided benefits will be available to immigrants, how we can integrate those coming from less advanced countries into a complex society, and how we will keep away people who want to destroy us. Many things have changed since my grandparents came to America around 1905. Our policies need modifying to deal with the changes. The answer is not a simple choice between letting immigrants in or not letting them in. It is not a choice between building a wall or not building a wall. There are two difficult aspects to this situation. Idealistically, should we or should we not drastically restrict immigration? Pragmatically, what system can we put in place to achieve the best outcome in either case?

Resolving this problem is not going to happen in our current political climate.

Here's a humorous and human TQM story. The president of Allied, who is a great guy named Steve, and I were visiting our branch manager in his office. A call came in for Steve, and he sat at the manager's desk to take the call. When he hung up, Steve asked the manager, Stan, for a diet soda. I knew from the smirk on Steve's face that he was up to something. Stan smacked himself in the head with the palm of his hand and said, "Damn, I forgot." What he forgot was to use his own system for not forgetting to get something done.

Stan's system consisted of the following:

People: Stan.
Process: Record things to do, look at the list periodically, do the things, and cross them off the list when done.
Technology: Desk calendar and pencil.

Note the way I did the layout. The "system" includes all three elements, but I put "process" between "people" and "technology" because "process" unites them. All three elements of a system are necessary to achieve the desired outcome. In this case, the desired outcome was to make a good impression on the big boss. I will add that everyone had a good laugh. We were a team.

There are three points here. First, it adds clarity to show the difference between two words that are often used interchangeably: system and process. Second, it shows that a system will fail if any element fails. Third, it demonstrates that working as a team is more fun than working in a culture where conflict is the norm.

We need to get things done. TQM is a useful tool that can make

America more productive if we use it the right way and in the right circumstances. TQM works under the following conditions:

- You start with an objective or mission statement.
- You incorporate modern and proven ideas about human nature so that a team of capable and motivated individuals working together can use a methodical approach to produce a suitable outcome, an approach that frequently borrows the best practices of others.
- You celebrate after a win and move on to tackle the next important issue you are facing.

Neither TQM nor any other approach can succeed without an agreed upon objective. TQM will not make a bad idea work or overcome ignorance, corruption, or deceit. As McGregor says, "The ingenuity of the average worker is sufficient to outwit any system of controls devised by management."[12] As an example, security officers sometimes carry a watchman's clock. It is in a leather case with a strap for carrying it like a purse, and it's about the size of a purse. In many situations, the property owner's insurance company stipulates the need for a security guard. The insurance company wants someone checking the building frequently, when it is otherwise empty, and looking for fire or other destructive events, such as a broken water line. There are key-stations located around the premises. As the officer tours the property, when he comes to a key-station, he inserts a metal key with a number on it and turns the key. It leaves an impression on a tape showing the time the officer was at that place in the building. The security manager for the facility removes the tape from the clock once a week. It is kept as proof for the insurance company that the building is being patrolled as required. Some "ingenious" officers bring a screwdriver on the first round of an eight-hour shift, turn the keys, and then unscrew the keys from the wall and take all of the keys back to their base. They "make the next six rounds" while sitting in a comfortable spot. On the last round of the shift, they put the keys back on the wall.

There will always be people who try to beat the system. If the system is well designed and the culture is right, few will try and almost all of them will be caught. No system will be perfect. There are three goals: create a system that is better than the one in place, make it the best you can, and establish a mechanism to improve it.

TQM preaches the importance of continuous improvement for every system. TQM itself has been and will continue to be improved. In the late 1980s and the 1990s, a method of doing things better, especially in a manufacturing environment, was introduced. It is known as "Lean Manufacturing."[13] TQM is an inherent part of Lean Manufacturing. Both emphasize the importance of building the right relationships among employees and managers. Both examine the same three elements of a system: people, process, and technology. The principles of TQM are solid. The more you learn about TQM, the more you will be able to use new ideas that spring from TQM.

———

The American automobile industry learned a hard lesson: TQM is a better way to do things, but it is not easy to practice. It requires a different culture, one built on teamwork, mutual respect, and trust. Experiment with applying TQM principles in your personal life. Stop contracting for work only on a price basis. Think of the time and frustration you will save if you build a relationship with those that you select to do work around your home and use them routinely rather than always shopping around. Give them a sense of pride of workmanship. Apply TQM to politics, too. Those who present themselves as the low-bidder, because they will keep your taxes low, are also probably the low performers. Those who are obnoxious and braggarts are not team players and will produce conflict rather than compromise. Changing the way things are done in government will also be hard to do, but we cannot hold onto the past and watch our society continue to deteriorate.

Maslow's Hierarchy of Needs [3]

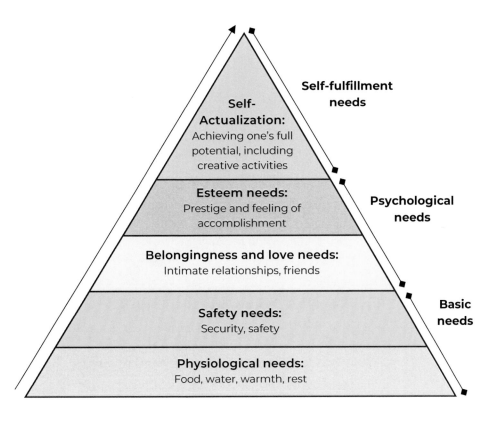

Selected Quotes

"Man is a wanting animal—as soon as one of his needs is satisfied, another appears in its place. This process is unending. It continues from birth to death."

"An objective without a plan is a dream."

"Most teams are not teams at all but merely collections of individual relationships with a boss. Each individual vying with the others for power, prestige, and position."

"Above all, it is necessary to recognize that knowledge cannot be pumped into human beings the way grease is forced into a machine. The individual may learn; he is never taught."

"Delegation means that he will concern himself with the results of the activities and not with the details of their day-to-day performance. This requires a degree of confidence in them which enables him to accept certain risks. Unless he takes risks, there will be no delegation."

–Douglas McGregor[12]

"You will either step forward into growth or you will step back into safety."

"All of life is education and everybody is a teacher and everybody is forever a pupil."

"If you only have a hammer, you tend to see every problem as a nail."

"What is necessary to change a person is to change his awareness of himself."

"The only happy people I know are the ones who are working well at something they consider important."

"One's only failure is failing to live up to one's own potential."

"The story of the human race is a story of men and women selling themselves short."

–Abraham Maslow[14]

Chapter 6

Election System Results

T he first five chapters dealt in general terms with problem-solving techniques and specifically, the application of a newer model of how to get things done called TQM. We took a fairly deep dive into some ways to evaluate human behavior because people are a critical element in getting anything accomplished. Their personalities must be suitable for the job they are expected to perform.

After some history, we will apply the material to our current system for placing people in public office at the highest level of our government. As Vice President Kamala Harris pointed out, electing someone to a public office is in essence a hiring process. We will explore the results of the selecting/hiring system.

The colonization of the North American continent is more

complex than you might remember from school. In 1565, the Spanish, not the English, were the first to establish a colony in what is now Florida.[2] The first English settlement was in Virginia in 1587, but it failed.[3] In 1606, King James I signed a charter allowing the start of colonialization. The next English settlement, also in Virginia, began on December 20, 1606. Named after the king, it became Jamestown. Of the five hundred original settlers, only sixty-one survived past 1610.[4] In 1607, the Dutch settled in what is now New York City. It was first called New Amsterdam. In 1608, the French came, followed by groups from Sweden and Germany. Later, even the Russians got involved and made claim to land on the northwest coast of the continent.[5]

By 1775, the date used for the start of the American Revolution, much had changed on both sides of the Atlantic. There were thirteen distinct geographic areas that were colonies of Great Britain. England had united with Scotland and Wales to become Great Britain by 1707.[6] The population in the colonies was about 4,000,000.[7] The King of Great Britain was King George III.[8] A considerable number of Americans, but by no means all, were fed up with British rule. They had exhausted all options except to revolt. They did.

The Declaration of Independence was signed on July 4, 1776, so that date is considered our official date of separation, but we were actually in limbo from 1775 until 1783, when the war ended. During that limbo period, if the British had won the war, we would not have become independent. It could have happened later, but we wouldn't now be setting off fireworks on July 4th.

Thomas Jefferson went to great lengths to lay out all of the grievances the colonies had against the British in the Declaration of Independence. It lists eighteen grievances, one of which has nine separate issues. It says the colonies had not disregarded their obligations to Britain and that they had tried every reasonable approach to resolve their disenchantment with their governmental predicament. In TQM parlance, he is saying the system was not producing the results needed, attempts to fix the system have been tried and failed, and there was only one choice: to create an entirely new system of governance that excluded British involvement.

If we take a hard and deep look at our current election system, a long list of issues indicates we have a major problem.

The system currently in place has done the following:

- Put individuals in the oval office who are suitable for a system that is failing us, one unsuitable for efficient, productive governance.

Much has changed in our country and the world over the last fifty years, but we have not kept up with those changes in the way our government conducts its business. Our leaders, rather than solving problems, have been creating problems.

- Put into the House of Representatives several people who are such extremists that they participated in the assault on the Capitol.

Elected officials on the far left or the far right control politics, and the majority of Americans are unrepresented. Such individuals are frequently unable and unwilling to compromise. Extremists have an all-or-nothing approach. Politicians with a middle-of-the-road view are much more likely to give a little to get things accomplished.

- Created a Senate so divided and acrimonious that little or nothing positive is accomplished.

The two-party tradition of blind loyalty to the party, selfish showboating by prestige-seeking senators to gain power within their own party, and disregard for what is right and best for the country is routine.

- Put individuals in power who are self-centered brawlers, expecting them to be unselfish members of a team working for the good of others.

I will return to the DISC method of behavioral analysis covered in Chapter 5. To reach high public office in this country, you must have a high dominance quotient. You must prefer and operate well in an unfriendly environment. We have become conditioned to expect and enjoy a good brouhaha when our politicians engage with one another or the media. It makes good theater, but no good comes from the bickering. It produces broken relationships, gridlock, and waste.

- Negated attempts to patch up system-wide failure with changes in people, process, or technology that have not solved and cannot solve the problem.

Deming made a point that if you put a good person in a bad system, the bad system wins. We have put a few good people in a bad system, and they have survived. We have put some other good people in a bad system, and the system has overpowered them. We have also put some people in the system who should never have been there in the first place. They thrive in a system that meets their personal needs without doing anything for the majority of Americans.

- Forced potentially dedicated public servants to adopt goals and the means to achieve those goals that conform to the extremist vision of the dominant political parties.

Even when individuals who are not extremists seek public office, the party they align with pushes them toward the extremes. Individuals must align themselves with a party if they want to get elected. Only a select few have been able to rise above this situation. Most were or have been around a long time and earned a reputation that enabled them to be the exception to the rule. The late Senator John McCain was such an individual.

- Made money all-important.

If you enter politics and have already established widespread name recognition, you need a ton of money to get elected. If you start with little or no name recognition, you need ten tons of money. Here are a few names of people who were elected to high office who started after they had already established a name for themselves: George Washington (general), Ulysses Grant (general), Dwight Eisenhower (general), Ronald Reagan (actor), John McCain (prisoner of war), Arnold Schwarzenegger (actor), Sony Bono (entertainer), Tommy Tuberville (college football coach), Mark Kelly (astronaut), and Donald Trump (businessman, reality TV star). In the two races for the Senate in Georgia in 2020-2021, about a billion dollars were spent in the general election in November and the runoff election in January.[9] The contest was critical because it could give the Democrats control of both chambers in Congress. Of the four contenders, the lowest net worth came in at about $800,000,[10] but he had some name recognition. The bulk of the money came from parties and special-interest groups across the country. Contributors were buying access and influence. Ultimately, all Americans pay the bill. Special-interest groups want something that is especially advantageous to them and that the bulk of Americans are not willing to support. Their payoff comes from increasing their chances to get what they want.

For profit-oriented enterprises, donations to political campaigns are one of the costs of doing business, and that cost eventually gets passed on to the customers: U.S. taxpayers.

- Been so character challenging that it turns away the people we really need in office.

We run off many good prospects. Some shy away from politics because they don't want to sell their souls to attract the money they need to participate in a campaign that lasts a year or more. Some are unwilling to subject themselves and their loved ones to living in a fishbowl. Some find the prospect of repeating the same message repeatedly for months unappealing. Some don't want to besmirch the reputation of others. Some don't want to endure having others denigrate them and their family members. Some potentially good politicians can't stand up to the type of background scrutiny their opponents and the media would put them through.

- Used new technology in the wrong ways.

Technology normally gets things done faster, cheaper, and better. Our current election system takes up more time than ever. The cost is mind-blowing, and the outcome is not better. With modern technology, we air our dirty laundry for the whole world to see. We employ sophisticated polling so that politicians can determine what we want to hear and then profess to offer exactly that. Social media can undermine an opponent without leaving a trace. During the Georgia senatorial runoff, Donald Trump sent me (and hundreds of thousands of others) messages every day.

- Diverted incumbents from doing the job they were hired to do.

Incumbents must go on the campaign trail, but does the trail have to be so long? Do they need to spend all that time and money to convince us that they deserve to be reelected or deserve to move to higher office?

- Turned voters away.

In the Georgia senatorial runoff election in 2021, 752,000 fewer people voted than did in the 2020 general election.[11] I was one of the ones who didn't vote. I was thoroughly disgusted with the entire sequence of events and the choices left. I could either vote for a candidate I didn't think represented my views, because none came close to doing so, or I could take small comfort in knowing I didn't help any get into office. I don't like peas or lima beans. I'd rather skip a meal or two than eat either. I believe that the other 751,999 citizens who didn't vote had similar frustrations. Why bother to make the effort to vote when you don't believe anything good will come from it?

- Been unnecessarily divisive.

If we made no other change than shortening the length of campaigns, it would reduce the damage. If we made other reasonable and logical changes, we could radically cut the dissension and bitterness that are byproducts of the system. As examples, the current system is focused on the negatives of the candidates and their parties, promoting fear rather than hope and failing to build trust and confidence.

- Damaged our image as a country and as Americans around the world.

I saved this subject for last. When I mentioned to some friends that our system damages America's image, I received pushback that surprised me. "Why should I care?" This response is noteworthy because it reflects the way things were done before TQM. It fails to recognize that things have changed and that we are now dependent on others. In Chapter 1, I raised the issue of relativity because it is so important. Three other "R" words are important: relationships, reliability, and respect.

The entities in a TQM organization interact in a manner entirely different from a pre-TQM organization. They care for the other members of the organization, not just themselves. We need to care about other countries and their citizens. They buy our products, use our services, allow us to place military bases on their soil, finance our debt, provide us with necessary resources, and so on. We need strong relationships around the world, but we can't form or maintain them if we don't care about our partners and what they think of us.

When customers evaluate the quality of a product or service, they place the most importance on reliability. They want a product or service to do what it promised to do. We have to care whether other countries view us as reliable. If they doubt our commitment or ability to live up to our military obligations or pay our debts, we are in a world of hurt.

People who are respected can get things done, a principle that motivates Nike to pay respected athletes millions to wear their apparel. It also explains why the millions disappear if the athlete loses respectability. Respect also helps organizations and countries get things done. For countries, those accomplishments are big, like settling international disputes or fighting terrorism. We definitely should care whether our election fiascos cause us to lose respect around the world.

Allow me to clear up one final point before moving on. I am an advocate of the concept "If it ain't broke, don't fix it." Our election system is broken beyond repair. We need a new system that incorporates the best ideas. I am dwelling on TQM because it is a great starting point. It is a new and better way to do things.

With grievances, Thomas Jefferson clearly did a better job than I just did. He came up with eighteen, and I have been able to come up with only thirteen. His eighteen, like my thirteen, are not the problem. They are the symptoms of a problem. If we cannot accept the fact that a problem exists and is serious enough that we must solve it, then we have an even bigger problem.

Let me brighten the mood with some humor. A middle-aged man goes to see his doctor.

Doctor: "Your age is catching up with you. You take forever to do what you should be able to do in no time, and even then, you make a mess of things."

Man: "I want a second opinion."

Doctor: "Okay, you still believe that might makes right, and you use your smart phone only to make telephone calls. Try to get into teamwork and take full advantage of the technology available to you. Your life will improve and you will make life better for all those who depend on you. "

Well, I am not Henny Youngman, but I hope I have succeeded in stimulating your thinking.

Our election system is not specified in the Constitution. More than anything, it is built on traditions that go back hundreds of years. Over time, we have added to the system, but we have rarely subtracted, and we have never taken a hard look at the whole system and attempted a major overhaul. If the election system were working to our satisfaction, there would be no need to make big changes, but that is not the case. We hear so much about how divided the nation is, and there is a great deal of talk about addressing the problem, but the division is not the problem. It is a result of our bad election system that spews out discord. Our election system is one of the major producers of a divided population, and the only way it can change is with a change to the system. Without a sound plan to enact change, we are dreaming.

If we can accept that a problem worthy of our attention is in front of us, the next step is to define that problem. Here is my attempt, but for the best possible definition, it should be a team effort of individuals from varying experiences, ethnicities, and disciplines.

Over many years, our election system has evolved into a collection of subsystems that no longer merge into an efficient and effective means to allow citizens to put people in office who are best suited to serve the needs of all Americans. We now have greater knowledge of human behavior and far superior technology that we should incorporate into a system that is cheaper, faster, and better. We should strive to achieve the following specific goals:

- Attract people suitable to the job.
- Minimize the potential for divisiveness.
- Remove money raising from the process.
- Develop a meaningful way to rank individual performance.
- Diminish the power of the political parties.
- Reward compromise and discourage obstruction.
- Constantly make changes to keep the system up to date and steadily improving.

It is a huge undertaking, but it is necessary and doable.

There is one element of our system that must never change. The citizens of America must retain the right to participate fully in hiring those who will represent and lead them. We deserve a system that produces results that steadily improve the quality of life for all Americans. We have the brainpower and technology to make it happen. We have to set our minds to the task, be willing to accept both change and compromise, look back at what our best leaders warned us about, and borrow the best ideas from around the world. Citizens will be much more inclined to vote if they have desirable choices instead of the lesser of two evils and if they believe the system is effective and fair.

If I go out to eat and the restaurant offers two specials, steak or lobster, I'd much prefer the steak, but if only lobster is left, I am okay with the lobster. Just don't serve it with peas or lima beans.

Voters will continue to have undesirable choices until we change our election system. You can help do that by not voting for those who exhibit deplorable behavior. And if a politician makes promises that sound too good to be true, they probably are. You are hearing a sales pitch that is a winner for the politician, his party, and the special interests that fund them. The losers are the majority of Americans. Our goal is an outcome where there are many more winners than losers.

Selected Quotes[12]

"Presidents are selected, not elected."

"An election cannot give a country a firm sense of direction if it has two or more national parties which merely have different names but are alike in their principles and aims."

"The value of love will always be stronger than the value of hate. Any nation...which employs hatred eventually is torn to pieces by hatred."

–Franklin Roosevelt

Chapter 7

Hiring/Selecting

"The supreme quality of leadership is integrity." [1]

–Dwight Eisenhower

T he Atlanta Falcons Football Team was looking for a new head coach—something it does fairly regularly. In professional sports, win/loss records let team owners know when their system is not producing the results they want. Technology in the game is standard, and the head coach is responsible for the processes used to train, practice, and play. When losses regularly exceed wins, the head coach is one of the two people typically fired. The other is the general manager, if he is heavily involved in player selection. As I recall—and it's hard to keep track because it has happened so many times—in the case I am referring to, the team was replacing only the head coach.

Management announced its new hire, a head coach from another team. Later, at a meeting of team owners, the owner of the Atlanta Falcons talked to the owner of the team that the head coach used to manage. The old owner told the new owner, "I can understand why you hired him; he interviews very well." In recruiting jargon, that statement is basically a kiss of death. The old owner was telling the new owner that they had both made a mistake because they measured the candidate's potential to perform as a football coach by evaluating his ability to interview. The hire did not produce acceptable results, and he was fired again. The individual interviewed well again and was hired by another team. That situation did not work out either. He then became a football commentator on TV, which he did well because he could talk a good game.

Placing the right people in the right job is a learned skill. It is not something you can do well by just doing what feels natural. Many individuals involved in hiring rely on silly myths and their allegedly innate ability to judge someone. They think they have the perfect reference system—themselves. The higher you have progressed in responsibility, it would seem, the better you become at all things involved in operating your business, including hiring. This thinking can lead to costly mistakes.

Senior managers who never worked in Human Resources make their share of errors when they take control of filling an important position. They frequently make bad decisions because they have just enough knowledge to muddle the process. The football team owners discussed at the opening of the chapter made a common mistake. They gave far more importance to interview skills than appropriate. Below are three true stories dealing with interviewing. All impart valuable lessons.

The first two stories deal with a widely accepted myth about the significance of eye contact during an interview. If only it were not a myth, interviewing and hiring would be a lot easier.

Here's the first story. Allied Security was asked to come to the rescue of an IRS complex where the security contractor on site had defaulted. The gigantic complex had dozens of round-the-clock security posts, and all of the officers carried weapons, so the position involved lots of extra screening and training. Two full-time IRS security administrators were on site, the head of security and the assistant. As the contractor, we were required to provide an on-site manager to oversee our employees. We put a temporary manager on-site while we looked internally for a manager to fill that role permanently. We identified someone who had been thoroughly screened and was completing a training program for branch managers. I flew with him from Atlanta to Boston to meet with the IRS security manager. He reviewed the man's background and interviewed him for about forty-five minutes. He indicated that we had made a good choice but wanted his assistant manager to spend a few minutes with the candidate.

The assistant came back in less than five minutes, went into the manager's office, and closed the door. When the door was opened a few minutes later, the manager asked me to come in and close the door. He informed me that his assistant felt that they could not work well together because our man did not make good eye contact during their time together. The manager told us to find someone else. This case was one where I bit my tongue and repeated to myself that the customer is always right. It was bad enough that both managers focused on one tiny aspect of human behavior instead of doing what trained recruiters do: look at the total person. Also, their reaction to poor eye contact was flawed. Not looking someone in the eyes can sometimes be a good sign. The value of a particular behavior is relative to the job, as the second story shows.

I was visiting a branch that was interviewing candidates to fill a branch secretarial position. A woman had applied for the job. I sat in for a minute to observe. After the candidate left, I asked the interviewer what he thought. He made several appropriate remarks and then said, "I really liked the way she made good eye contact throughout the interview."

I asked, "Why is that?" He gave me a confused look.

I knew what he was thinking: "Everybody says eye contact is important. She exhibited good eye contact. Where did I go wrong?" I explained, "A branch secretary has security officers, predominately men, coming into the office all the time. Her primary duties are to type and prepare payroll. You need to look for an introverted person who loves her computer and her payroll journals. A truly introverted person will stare at her shoes during an interview. That's what you want. The one who makes good eye contact is more likely to be an extrovert and spend valuable time talking with anyone who will listen." I added, "But don't put too much weight on this single issue. Look at the total person, especially the applicant's prior work history."

The next story involves a CEO who liked to take part in hiring senior managers. He was a domineering individual and believed that all senior managers should be like him. The company used DISC to measure behavior, so he favored candidates with high dominance quotients. In the interview, he would slip from a friendly posture to one of confrontation and see how the candidate reacted. If the interviewee came right back at him, he approved. If the CEO could find a pattern of aggressive conduct in the person's work history, he was equally impressed.

Two problems existed in that scenario. First, the CEO was placing too much emphasis on one aspect of the individual rather than looking at the total person. The second and bigger problem was that his senior management team was not a team at all. It was a group of prima donnas all out for themselves. The culture was one of conflict.

Some people spend their entire careers selecting people to fill jobs. Human behavior is a complex area that merits years of study, and even professional recruiters still have much to learn. The more experience you have perfecting your skills at matching the right people with the right jobs, the better you can perform.

A recruiter once told me he judged character based on whether people salted their food before or after they tasted it. Hogwash!

To evaluate an interviewee correctly, you must know what you are seeking. A great talker is not always a great doer, but a great talker might make a great customer-relations person. No one person is right for every job, but you can fill more jobs correctly when you acknowledge that everyone has unique combinations of qualities and that there is someone for every job. The idea of relativity comes into play again. A job must be clearly defined, and the type of person who can best fill that job must also be clearly defined. The best indicator of future performance is past performance. It is not some myth about eye contact or the application of salt. To hire effectively, a proven system must be in place. Knowledgeable practitioners must run it using the best available technology and in the right way.

Before I talk about the first step in hiring—defining a position—I want to return to a statement I made about there being a person for every job. Many people have a narrow view of the jobs that people are willing to perform. Their reference point is their station in life and the station of those around them. I, like everyone else, have said, "I could never do that job." But after spending twenty-five years in a business where I visited every kind of organization and saw all types of jobs, I never say, "We will never find someone to do that job." People are vastly different in needs, traits, and behavioral patterns. The right person can be found to fill any job.

Allied provided security for a paint factory that was more than a hundred years old. It was an unpleasant place to work because huge mixing containers of paint had spilled all over the floors and equipment. The smelly facility was hot. Our officers had to conduct a tour every hour. The tour was so long that when they had completed one round, the time to start the next was almost immediate. They were there alone. Our best officer there was a chess master. He had sacrificed almost everything in his life to practice and play competitive chess. He lived in a rundown apartment within walking distance of the paint factory. He had no car. He shared the apartment with two other men. He worked no more than twenty-four hours a week to minimize his time away from chess. He preferred to work two shifts of twelve hours, rather than three shifts of eight hours, to reduce the walks to and from work. I visited his apartment once. I play a little chess, but his devotion to the game was way beyond what most would consider normal. He had chessboards in three rooms and a game in progress on each board. He explained that one board was for opening moves, the second was for the middle game, and the third board was for end-game practice. He asked me to make a move on one of the boards. I did. He said it was a good move, but he was probably just being nice to the boss. His job filled his need for income; his lifestyle met his basic needs and allowed him to self-actualize. He wanted to be the best chess player he could be.

Another site where we placed security officers was a big garbage dump. One lone officer was on duty. He was there to stop unauthorized dumping. He sat in or near a small guard booth. If a vehicle came in and tried to dump garbage after hours, he was to chase it away. If his efforts didn't work, he recorded the license plate number. Because of the garbage smell and the environment, the dump manager didn't care how the officer's uniform looked or whether the officer bathed. All the manager cared about was whether the officer dealt with unauthorized dumping. The officer was also allowed to bring a small portable TV and a pellet gun to work. He could pass time by watching TV and shooting rats.

An introvert rejuvenates by being alone. An extrovert finds vitality by being with others. Our security officer at the dump did fine by himself and where people were not put off by his lack of hygiene.

In Vietnam, one of my unit's responsibilities was to maintain an important road. A convoy of trucks made one back-and-forth trip a day on the road to move manpower and supplies. My unit, along with others, had to provide some of the personnel to staff the convoy. One vehicle in the convoy was a flatbed truck carrying a fifty-caliber machine gun. It fired bullets about a half inch in diameter and well over an inch long. It could fire about a thousand rounds a minute. A person shot in the shoulder by that weapon would probably have his entire shoulder blown off. My unit frequently provided the guy who operated that gun. He stood on that platform, very much exposed, and scanned both sides of the road, watching and waiting for an ambush. His life was at risk because he would be one of the first targets of ambushers. One soldier always volunteered for that job. He was willing to risk his life to get a chance to shoot at enemy soldiers. The issue here is not the mental state of this man. The issue is that recruiters need people to do all kinds of jobs, and the right people to fill those jobs are out there. The average person might find some jobs repugnant, but people exist who, for whatever reason, are willing and able to do those jobs.

Let me explain how I got into the recruiting business. I had been with Allied for about one and a half years after leaving P&G. After fourteen months as a branch manager, I was promoted to regional vice president and invited to attend my first management advisory board meeting in Pittsburgh. In my eighteen months with the company, I often received memos that changed our internal telephone directory to reflect a new branch manager in one office or another. With only fifteen branch offices, far too many important management changes were taking place. I commented at my first meeting that the management changes were an indication of a problem. When asked what I thought should be done, I answered, "We should look at the system we use to hire and train branch managers." Within thirty seconds, I was assigned the additional responsibility of being the company's personnel manager.

The senior management group consisted of the president, two executives who were CPAs, and two regional vice presidents. The other vice president was a former police officer. The founder and president was a former military policeman and door-to-door encyclopedia salesman. Don't sell him short. He built a business that he sold for $100 million dollars and became the chairman of the Pittsburgh Port Authority. He could sell anything to anybody. He got things done. He surrounded himself with people with the capabilities he lacked. He knew when to get involved, and he knew when to step back and let his subordinates do what needed to be done.

Suddenly the head of a nonexistent personnel department, I reached out to people in recruiting at P&G. I asked how they operated their hiring system. Because they were TQM trained, they were willing to help. Allied Security was not a P&G competitor, so if we became better at what we did, everybody benefited. Who knew? It might one day help Allied deliver better security services to P&G. The P&G recruiters told me their system was built on the program outlined in *Tested Techniques of Personnel Selection* by Dr. Robert N. McMurry. I bought the book, read it, and was blown away. Even though I had been the one recruited several times, I had no idea how much went on behind the scenes. What surprised me most was that good recruiters were as concerned about measuring what I *would* do as they were with what I *could* do. Character mattered as much as competence.

As you can see, when I started recruiting in 1974 with Allied Security, I followed one of the principles of TQM. I searched for a system someone else created and found effective.

I learned a great deal from systems already in place. Here are some of the highlights.

The starting point when hiring is a job description and person specifications. These items used to be separate but are now combined. I will discuss them individually.

A job description is a comprehensive summary of what the new hire is expected to do and the circumstances under which it will be done. Below is a list of areas and a brief explanation, if needed, for filling a hypothetical position for a regional vice president of sales for a security service provider.

Position: Regional Vice President of Sales

Location: Atlanta based*

Travel: Frequent overnight travel required**

Organizational Position: Reports to the national sales and marketing vice president and has seven branch salespeople reporting to him/her. Is on the same level as the regional operations manager.

Duties:

1. Participates in the selection and training of all new salespeople
2. Monitors the day-to-day activities of salespeople
3. Helps with the preparation of all sales proposals, especially pricing
4. Regularly accompanies salespeople when making sales calls and presentations
5. Ensures that information about customers and potential customers is recorded
6. Has other duties

Compensation:
>Salary $ _____
>Commission $ _____
>Bonus $ _____
>401(k)
>Health Insurance
>Travel Reimbursement
>Vacation Policy
>Etc.

Availability:
>Fill opening in fifteen to sixty days
>*Location is at the top of the list because it is a potential deal breaker. If a candidate does not want to be based in Atlanta, further discussion is wasted.
>** Travel can also be an insurmountable hurdle.

Preparing a job description and the person specifications, which we will get to in a moment, is a team effort. In this instance, the following people participate: corporate personnel manager, vice president of sales and marketing, other regional sales vice presidents, and the corporate vice president of operations. These individuals will be most helpful in defining the character aspects they want in the person hired. The top-rated regional salespeople will complete forms that define their own character. All four will fill out a form that projects the character traits they think are best for the job. The personnel manager will combine all of the data and determine the character of strong performers and the character as defined by the job forms. These two things should be similar. The vice president of operations is involved because his regional operations managers and branch managers will interface with the hire daily. They must work as a team. The operations people must deliver the service that is sold. If they cannot, then everybody loses.

Below is a sample "person specifications" for this position. First are those under the heading of "Competence," followed by those under the heading of "Character." Some specifications might appear in both.

Competence (Can Do)

IQ: 110 to 140 as measured by the ABC Test

Writing Skills: Strong, as shown in the application questionnaire

Work Experience:
- Minimum of four years as service
- salesperson
- Minimum of five years as sales manager in a business selling services
- Familiarity with XYZ sales training program
- Familiarity with MNO customer sales activity recording system
- Knowledgeable of TQM and a good team player
- Sold a service, such as janitorial services, to a similar customer base
- Not under a non-compete agreement with a security service in Southeast

Education: BS or BA

Verbal Skills: Excellent communicator

Appearance: Professional dress and grooming

Criminal History: None

Character (Will do):

    Location: Now in Atlanta or willing to move to Atlanta

    Availability: Within no more than sixty days

    Compensation: Last position income $ _____

    DISC Scores: _____

    Values: _____

The combined job description and person specifications represent the employer's wish list. Job candidates have their own wish lists. The entire system is designed to bring the two together in a mutually beneficial relationship. If either party engages in deception, the relationship will probably end badly.

Armed with a clear job description, which from this point on includes person specifications, the recruiter is ready for the next phase in the overall system of hiring. He must develop and search through a body of talent to find someone suitable for the position. If possible, he will look within his own organization. Doing so has three advantages: he can better evaluate the individual's past performance, others in the organization will see that good performance is recognized and rewarded, and the financial cost is lower. Let's assume he has looked internally and decided he will look outside his organization.

For illustrative purposes, I have changed the position from mid-level manager to entry-level manager. I made this switch because the search technique involved has a broader application than the one used for higher management. I will start by describing what I encountered when I was planning to leave the Army in late 1969.

When I was looking for a job in the civilian world, I came in contact with an outfit called Lendman Associates. Lendman dealt exclusively with junior officers leaving the service who were job hunting. It set up career conferences and invited employers looking for managers and officers looking for new careers. A typical conference might have fifteen companies, such as Shell Oil, Kimberly-Clark, Arthur Anderson, Pepsi, or P&G. Maybe three hundred applicants attended. Each brought a stack of résumés. Every employer's representative made a two-minute presentation to all attendees about the company, its job openings, and appropriate qualifications. After all of the employers made their remarks, attendees could go to a table to speak with a recruiter from that organization.

I attended a conference in Washington, D.C. I talked to about six companies. I waited my turn to get to the table. I handed over my résumé and had a few minutes to determine whether there was interest on both sides. If there was mutual interest, we scheduled a half-hour interview for the following day. At some tables, applicants were given a questionnaire to fill out and leave with the recruiter that evening. Some applicants were asked to attend a group session, before their interview, that would involve taking a test.

I later learned that a lot went on behind the scenes. The recruiters went to the conference the day before the applicants. They went to a hospitality suite where they could screen every applicant's résumé. They had a specific, written job description for each position they were trying to fill. When you screen three hundred résumés, you have to know exactly what you want and what you don't want. "Don't wants" are easy knockouts. The applicant wants a sales job in New York. You are looking for an accountant in St. Louis. Out it goes. If you see a match between a job description and a résumé, you tell the representative from Lendman to send that applicant a message to come to your table the next day.

I set up thirty-minute appointments the next day of the job fair with IBM, Babcock & Wilcox Construction, and P&G. IBM scheduled me to take a test. The construction and engineering company gave me a one-page, word-choice questionnaire to complete and drop off at its suite that evening. I flunked the IBM test. IBM was hiring programmers, and apparently other candidates demonstrated higher aptitude. At the time, I was disappointed. Later, I realized that this outcome was favorable. It kept me from pursuing a job for which I was poorly suited and at which I probably would have failed. I learned later that the questionnaire I completed for Babcock & Wilcox compared my behavioral pattern (DISC) to the DISC profiles of those who had been good at the jobs where the company had openings.

When I became a recruiter, I used many types of behavior analysis tools. These tools are part of character determination. There are vehicles to measure honesty, psychotic behavior, and many other types of good and bad conduct. The forms we used measured areas such as introversion vs. extroversion, aggressive style vs. passive style, etc. Many inexperienced recruiters focus almost completely on the competence of an individual and neglect the character side or assume that competence in one field translates to competence in any field. Another common recruiting error is to assume that because you are good at your job, if you hire people like you, they will be good at their job. This rationale is flawed. The job you're hiring for is probably different from your job and requires a different type of person.

I visited both P&G and Babcock & Wilcox. I took more tests. P&G gave me an IQ test. I endured interviews with groups of screeners and individual interviews with middle managers and plant managers. Never was I confronted with another candidate for the same job or even told about my competition. Babcock & Wilcox and I came to the same conclusion. We were not right for one another.

P&G made an offer and invited my wife and me back. This time, the company was in "sales" mode. P&G wanted me to accept the offer and knew it might have competition. We were escorted by managers who had been with P&G for about a year. Talking with them and their wives allowed us to determine whether P&G had lived up to their expectations. Everyone treated us like royalty. We ate at top restaurants and were shown what Cincinnati had to offer. I accepted the offer, moved my family from Virginia, and started my civilian career in Cincinnati. It was a good move.

The best job description you can design is of little help if you can't find a source of potentially qualified people to pursue the position. You might not be able to attract interest because of your compensation package, location, screening techniques, or culture.

In the private security industry, we regularly heard, "Why don't you screen your people better?" Screening was not our problem. Our problem was that we could not attract enough well-qualified people to pick the best people for the job. We had a hard time finding enough individuals to meet the minimum requirements. Why didn't we make changes? The reason was that the customers said they wanted one thing but had systems that only allowed them to get something else. Most used the low-bid system to award their contracts. They prepared a request for a bid that was comparable to the perfect job description. To get a suitable contractor, more is required. Writing great bid specifications, like preparing a great job description, is a good start, but there is much more to do. You have to be able and willing to compensate the contractor sufficiently to deliver what you say you want instead of what your budget will permit.

A similar situation prevails in our system for hiring politicians. The system is so arduous and degrading to the type of people we need in office that those best suited for the job will not participate. Our system will perform as it has in the past until we adopt a system that has a defined objective and is structured to achieve that objective.

I have drawn a parallel between how the low-bid system fails us when we are picking a contractor and how our election system fails us when we are selecting a public servant. Next, I want to compare the way an organization such as P&G thins a pool of applicants to the way our election system performs the same task for the electorate.

In the recruiting of an entry-level supervisor at P&G, the recruiter had to narrow the prospects down from three hundred to two or three. The recruiter made the first cut when he invited only ten to twelve people for the thirty-minute interview at the job fair. The recruiter then cut the list down to about six and gave them applications to complete. If three applications came back, middle managers and possibly the plant manager screened them. A decision would then be made about who would be invited for a plant visit. After a full day and a half of interviews and comparisons with other candidates, the decision was made to extend an offer or to start another search.

A similar system narrows the field of politicians to the names that appear on ballots.

No one at the P&G plant saw the 290 candidates who were cut during the résumé review stage. The P&G recruiter decided whom to give applications. By the time the decision makers became involved, only two or three very similar candidates would remain if the recruiter had performed well and the system was working as intended. With our current election system, voters make the final decision about politicians. Voters become involved only at the end of the proceedings, after party leaders and special-interest groups have cut the field to those they will support with endorsements and money. Here is where the system fails. The voters, who are customers, are the victims of a system that, like the low-bid system in contracting, generates a poor outcome. This system runs off candidates who are suitable and presents us with the remainder. Voters are stuck in a self-perpetuating quagmire:

a culture of conflict and selfishness, gridlock and waste, with no chance for anything different.

The customer is always right, but customers are not always equipped to do what is in their own interests. In many cases, the customer elects to believe in fairy tales and myths. Voters are easily misled by politicians who talk a good game and tell them they can have their cake and eat it, too. Devious salespeople make a great living by telling customers exactly what they want to hear. Many companies have been fooled into hiring the wrong people, and many employees have gone to work for companies that misrepresented the job to them. We cannot eliminate these problems, but we can establish a good system that will give us a fighting chance to achieve more good outcomes than bad. Customers—in this case, voters—deserve a system that gives them two good choices rather than two bad ones.

In the chapter on TQM, we discussed the entirely different way that the entities of an organization interact. The best way to understand this interaction is to realize that traditional labels can cause confusion. In TQM, each party is a customer, and each party is a service provider. The company treats their customers and their employees as "customers." The employees treat the customer and the company as their "customers." And the customer, as strange as it sounds, treats the company and their employees as "customers."

Think of a simple situation. A homeowner wants to hire a painting contractor. The homeowner is doing the hiring. When the contractor is on board, the homeowner becomes a customer. But the contractor is now the homeowner's customer, too. The homeowner has to provide electricity, bathroom facilities, and so on. A savvy customer knows he will get better performance if he treats his contractor well.

In the political arena, voters participate in the hiring process by screening the candidates and casting their ballot. When the electee takes office, the voter becomes the customer, or at least they would if the system were working. The politician is supposed to serve his constituents. In return, citizens should treat politicians well by respecting them for the extremely difficult problems they face. Traditional labels can be used in TQM but with the understanding that they can be ambiguous in an environment where productive teamwork is the objective.

Hiring systems and the U.S. election system have many similarities and some significant differences. Later, we will take what is transferable from hiring and apply it to elections, but we must make allowances for the differences.

A hiring system works from the top down. An election system is basically the reverse. During the hiring process, the higher up an individual is in an organization, the more power he has over the final hiring decision. The narrowing of candidates occurs at the low end of management, even though higher management helps prepare the job description. In the election system, the higher-ups do the narrowing, and the voters make the final choice.

Firms have clearly designated individuals or small groups of people who make the final decision. The whole system runs from the top, and the objective is well-defined. Higher managers want to fill a specific job with a person with the competence and character they believe is best suited to deliver the results they seek. The election system, however, has no leader. It follows practices that have evolved over hundreds of years without much consideration for efficiency or effectiveness. The system is unmanaged. It produces a result, but without leadership and change, the system tends to produce the same result. We repeat this activity a few years later, having changed nothing in the system that might have produced a better outcome. Deming said that managing by results is like driving when looking through the rearview mirror.

Deming didn't say the following, but he was probably thinking it: "Looking through the rearview mirror is a good way to go backwards, but not the right way to move forward."

Deming's comment brings up a semantic issue. He says that managing by results and objectives is not desirable, but he also says that we must measure the results of the system in place. There is a very fine distinction here. The simplest, but not complete, explanation is that if a system is not producing the desired results, you have to manage (i.e., be willing to change) the entire system. You cannot go and tell the people who are part of the system that their results are unsatisfactory and that they better get their act together. The results of a system need measuring to determine how well it is working. If the system is working fine, management should make sure it continues to work fine and improve it. If the system is not working well, it must be faulty, and management needs to look backwards for a time to see what went wrong and try to fix the problem. If they are consistently managing poor outcomes, they are not doing their job well. Management's job is to create systems that consistently produce good results.

In hiring, candidates are evaluated on competence and character. In the election system, a third element comes into play that frequently overrides all other considerations: ideals. Voters are frequently forced to choose between the ideals of the two major parties. This situation is unavoidable, but it could be better managed if we were not always pushed to the extremes of the two parties, if we reduced the stranglehold the parties have on the election system, and if we did not lose sight of the importance of character and competence. Voters can easily be misled by a politician who espouses lofty goals that are unreachable and designed to distract voters from tasks that can and need to be accomplished. The distance between ideals is a major reason for gridlock, divisiveness, and the waste produced by doing and undoing.

In hiring, if the system works well, folks making the final decision might look at two or more candidates who are so similar and so closely match the job description that the choice comes down to a tiny detail. In this situation, assuming the system has worked as intended, the decision makers can't go wrong. They might even decide to create an opening and hire both candidates. If only the same were the case during an election. Voters generally end up with two choices that are vastly different and often unappealing to the moderate majority.

The last difference between a hiring system and the election system is a sensitive one. In most organizations, the people assigned a role in hiring are knowledgeable and experienced. Those who are new to the role will have less influence on the outcome. As they participate and demonstrate the ability to contribute, their influence will increase. The same is not true with voters. All votes count the same, whether made by someone who has done extensive research on the candidates or someone who uses the talks-a-good-game method of evaluation. We can and should provide voters with the knowledge they need to make informed decisions. The best thing we can do, however, is to construct a system that gives the vast majority of voters a choice between two good candidates.

Hiring techniques give us a reference system that we can adapt to our election system. The power of the people at the bottom of the pyramid is an essential element of democracy and should remain, but new approaches would allow voters to maintain that power and still place the people we need in positions to represent and lead us. New ways require change, and change is good for both individuals and organizations.

―――――――

Readers can now move beyond the myths when selecting those who will be doing work for them as contractors, employees, or public servants. Think about the story involving the football coach and the owners of the three football teams. The common error was picking someone who interviewed well. They could not have paid much attention to past performance. Use the information in this chapter if you or a loved one is job hunting. The goal is a win-win relationship.

Selected Quotes[2]

"You need to have a collaborative hiring process."

–Steve Jobs

"Do not hire a man who does your work for money, but him who does it for the love of it."

–Henry David Thoreau

"Time spent on hiring is time well spent."

–Robert Half

"I am convinced that nothing we do is more important than hiring and developing people."

–Lawrence Bossidy

"If you think it's expensive to hire a professional, wait until you hire an amateur."

–Red Adair

Chapter 8

Rating Techniques

"Ninety-nine percent of leadership failures
are failures of character." [1]

–Norman Schwarzkopf

W e have been talking about "good" and "bad." These words are meaningless unless all parties concerned agree to what is good and what is bad. More importantly, we need a means to measure and compare things in a helpful way.

In sports, good individual performance is sometimes easy to measure and compare with an accepted standard. Golf is a great example. Scoring is easy. You count the number of strokes a player takes to get around a course. You can then compare that score with par, with your playing partners, and even the lowest round ever achieved on that course. All of these comparisons involve relativity.

In a sport such as figure skating, however, making comparisons and determining when one skater performs better than all of the others is more difficult. Nonetheless, it must be done and it is done.

Most professional, well-managed organizations have developed systems for evaluating individual performance. In this case, we are no longer talking about a means to score potential performance; we are talking about rating actual performance. We will examine the systems in place in the four organizations I have worked for, discuss the system used for elected officials, and see whether we can apply some of the techniques used by my former employers in the political arena.

When I entered the United States Military Academy at West Point in July 1961, I became an employee in the U.S. Army. As a cadet, I was paid to learn how to be an Army officer. West Point is sometimes referred to as a trade school because it turns out Army officers and basically nothing else. My salary was $111.11 a month. It was a year-round job. I had thirty days of leave in the summers but spent the rest of those summers engaged in military training. Upon graduating forty-seven months after entering, I automatically became a second lieutenant, and my salary doubled. Yes, to a whopping $222 a month. At that time, all graduates had a degree in engineering. The Academy was established to educate military engineers.

West Point had an elaborate system for measuring cadet performance. We were graded in three areas: academics, military bearing (leadership), and athletics. The school's mission statement included the following: "educate, train, and inspire the Corps of Cadets so that each graduate is a commissioned leader of character committed to the values of Duty, Honor, Country and prepared for a career of professional excellence and service to the Nation as an officer in the United States Army."[2]

The academy follows a Leader Development Program that focuses on character, academics, physical fitness, and military programs.

Few other institutions of higher learning pay much attention to character and physical fitness. Character is critical to leadership, so character development is part of the West Point experience. Cadets must follow the honor code and are subject to dismissal if they violate that code. A cadet cannot graduate if he cannot swim, do at least seven pull-ups, and complete other physical feats such as running a mile while wearing a military uniform, including combat boots, in a specified time. Both the character and the competence of graduates are relative to the job they will be expected to perform for as long as they stay in the Army.

At the end of a forty-seven-month stay, each cadet's overall performance determines his numerical standing in the class and his position in The Long Grey Line. My year-group started with about 900 students. About one-third of those who started did not complete the program. I was 124th in a graduating class of 596, making me the 25,609[th] graduate of the academy since its founding in 1802. It is interesting to note that General Douglas MacArthur stood first in his class[3] and General George Custer, the commander at Little Big Horn, where his unit was massacred, was last in his year-group.[4] This contrast is indicative of a performance evaluation system that appears to correlate with future job performance.

One of the ways of measuring leadership is particularly appropriate to our discussion. Cadets play a role in this system. In the early 1960s, there were about 2000 cadets at the academy. In round numbers, there were 20 companies of 100 cadets. Each company had twenty-five cadets from each of the four year-groups. There was a cadet chain-of-command. Cadets were assigned ranks from private to captain and responsibilities for overseeing others from zero to 2000. Rank and responsibilities were determined by year-group and leadership ratings. Seniors held the highest rank and were assigned responsibilities based on the evaluation of their leadership.

Leadership ratings were done by company. The twenty-five cadets who were seniors would rate those in their class and all three lower classes. The twenty-five juniors would rate their classmates and all those behind them, etc. For each year-group, the rater listed those being rated from one to twenty-five. He then had to explain why he put the people he did in the top two spots and the bottom two spots. These cadet ratings were an important part of the overall leadership rating system. The most responsible leadership position was that of brigade commander. He was the leader of the 2000-man Corps of Cadets.

The entire system used to educate cadets at West Point, including the leadership rating subsystem, seem to be working. I will use my class, the class of 1965, as an example. These three classmates held high rank within the Corps of Cadets: Dan, Paul, and Bob. Dan was number one in the class, Paul was number eighteen, and Bob was number forty. If the educational system at West Point and the rating system have value, there should be a correlation between their class rank and their performance after graduation. Dan became a general and finished his Army career as the superintendent at West Point. Paul was awarded the Medal of Honor. He was the commander of a company when it was attacked by a numerically superior Vietnamese force. His leadership and personal bravery during the battle was such that his own soldiers recommended him for that medal. Every year, he speaks to cadets at West Point and the Air Force Academy about leadership. Bob, who was fortieth in the class and was our brigade commander, has a building at West Point that bears his name. To provide relativity, some other buildings there bear these names: Washington, Eisenhower, Grant, and Pershing. He gave his life fighting for America. Virtually every graduate served at least one tour in Vietnam and many served two. More than twenty-five lost their lives in that war. Several were terribly injured. West Point's mission statement is, in part, to produce leaders "of character committed to the values of Duty, Honor, Country."

I consider my time in the regular Army a separate job because it was quite different from being at the Academy, as was the rating system. In the Army, every six months or at the end of each assignment, your boss and his boss prepared an officer efficiency report. They ranked you against your peers. If you were a company commander, the battalion commander and a group commander ranked you against other company commanders in their organizations. The reports were reviewed with you and then became a permanent part of your personnel file. Other things went into that file, such as letters of reprimand, class standing in Army courses you took, and medals awarded.

West Pointers right out of the academy were commonly viewed as inexperienced and immature. Many of them who entered the academy two weeks after graduating from high school found that, for the first time, they had the freedom to do things they could never do before. Some handled the freedom better than others.

I was one of the youngest members of my class and had not come from a military family, unlike many of my classmates. I also had a tendency to think outside the box and challenge authority if I saw something I thought was wrong. I ruffled some feathers, and it showed in some of my reviews. Regardless, I was promoted with my peers and received good efficiency reports for my time spent as a company commander in Vietnam. A good rating while in a command position in a war zone is especially important, but the rating system made it clear to me that I had to change if I wanted to achieve a high rank, or I would have to leave the Army. I chose to leave. The evaluation system was good for both parties. My almost nine years in the Army was educational and rewarding. I don't regret any part of it. The culture in the Army was not right for me, however, and I was not right for the Army.

I know P&G had a rating system, but I don't know the details. I saw evidence of the system at work. My first assignment was as a production supervisor. I replaced someone who must not have done well in the rating system because he was not leaving the company by choice. In my second assignment, I worked in the corporate security department, and my predecessor was also on his way out the door. Meanwhile, my first boss at P&G was promoted to a third-level management position. In my judgment, he was one of the best managers I have known. He went on to become a plant manager at a young age and would have moved even higher had he not succumbed to cancer in his forties.

At P&G, I worked with some wonderful people and was constantly learning. I chose to leave because I wanted more opportunities. I was willing to trade a safe position for a riskier one to get the chance to lead at a younger age. I went from a company with revenues of six billion dollars a year to one with revenues of six million dollars.

Within eighteen months at Allied Security, I was one of the five senior managers in the company. In setting up the personnel group at Allied, I put a rating system in place. The two key positions at the branch level were branch manager and branch salesperson. At every management advisory board meeting, we reviewed everyone in those two positions and ranked them from top to bottom. If those at the bottom were doing an acceptable job, nothing was done. If their performance was less than acceptable, they were scheduled for replacement. As we developed and fine-tuned our hiring and training programs, the need to terminate people steadily decreased.

Allied Security had two other rating systems tied to TQM. Because every business must focus on customer satisfaction, it must measure and rate customer service. First, we determined the most important thing to the majority of security-service users: "missed coverage." When a customer contracts for a security officer to be on duty twenty-four hours a day, seven days a week, the customer expects 168 hours of coverage each week and nothing less. The customer will not accept excuses, including debilitating illness. When a customer has coverage that starts every afternoon at four o'clock, the customer does not want to hear that the officer has been in a car accident or is stuck in traffic, especially if the customer representative can't leave work until an officer arrives. Knowing our customers' number-one priority, we set in place a system to monitor every instance of missed coverage company-wide, reporting it biweekly to all levels of management. The report told us how well we were meeting this expectation and enabled us to rank branch managers' performance in a vital area and in measurable terms.

TQM guru W. Edwards Deming would be appalled if I allowed you to think that we tried to manage the results and not the system. We evaluated every new contract to see whether we could manage it in a way to ensure we didn't miss coverage. Customers with continuous coverage, especially those with multiple guards on duty, were fairly easy to manage. The hardest accounts for which to prevent missed coverage were those with coverage that started at eight in the morning or four in the afternoon. Those start times occurred during heavy traffic periods and were difficult to meet with 100% consistency.

When we considered a contract far away from another contract location, we used several techniques to prevent missed coverage:

- We could schedule the officer to be at a location at three o'clock, even though coverage started at four o'clock. If the officer did not show up at three o'clock, we had an hour to send a supervisor.
- We could have an officer coming off duty at three

o'clock and traveling home stop by at 3:45 to give us a backup.

- We could have a field supervisor at the job at 3:45.
- We could opt not to take the contract. We preferred to turn down work that we could not confidently perform to a customer's satisfaction.

Another way we measured customer satisfaction was to send every customer a performance rating questionnaire every six months. It was a formal system of collecting and measuring performance. We also had informal means, such as monthly meetings with customers and periodic meetings with regional and corporate managers. Any expression of dissatisfaction resulted in the development of a plan to address and correct the source of dissatisfaction. Each year, we held a meeting attended by all branch managers and salespeople. We recognized and gave awards to managers who had done a great job satisfying their customers as measured by our two rating systems.

Earlier, I talked about sports, and I want to return to that subject. Sports are a microcosm of much larger and more complex areas of life. They are simpler to examine and provide valuable lessons. The higher the level of competition in any sport, and even games such as chess or bridge, the more analytical the approach is to managing the effort. In sports that involve a team of players, the better teams use many of the principles of TQM. Teamwork is the backbone of TQM, as it is in team sports. Teams measure performance and results in every way possible and then come up with a new way. If the performance is not what they need, they revise the training and the plays, and if necessary, the people involved, until they start winning more.

In sports, there is a fine line between measuring potential to perform and measuring why an athlete routinely outperforms everyone else. I was a gymnast in high school and college. I was better than average. My coach at West Point was the coach of the U.S. Olympic team, and we had members of the Olympic team working as coaches or training with us. The military draft was still in effect, and many world-class athletes joined the Army and got assigned to West Point so that they could coach and train. Soon after I graduated, the assistant tennis coach was Arthur Ash, who later became a world-famous tennis professional.

Training daily with top-notch gymnasts quickly made me realize I would never be among the elite of the sport. I had three uncorrectable problems. In gymnastics, part of the scoring is based on form, and one element of form is keeping your legs together. I could not keep my legs together because they were bowed.

Albert Einstein would appreciate my second problem because it was a matter of physics. One of my better events was the still rings. At the higher levels of competition on still rings, you have to do iron crosses. The iron cross move looks like a cross because you extend your arms straight out to the sides, parallel to the floor, while you hold your body in a vertical position. It is called the iron cross because of the position and because you must pump tons of iron to gain the strength necessary to hold that position for the required three seconds. In addition to bowed legs, I was born with longer arms than average for my height. The longer your arms, the more gravity works against you when doing iron crosses.

The first time I danced with my wife, she identified the third problem I had as a gymnast. I was rhythmically challenged. At the Olympic level, you have to perform in six events, and one of the six is the pommel horse, which is all about rhythm. If your rhythm is not well above average, you will never master that apparatus.

I will refer to another sport and another athlete and then apply it to rating systems. A swimming coach looked at a young boy and saw a potential world-champion swimmer. He was tall for a swimmer and had long arms, but of much greater importance, he had big feet. His potential was obvious and that coach turned Michael Phelps into one of the best swimmers ever.

Experts in their sports can spot talent at an early stage and identify limitations. Coaches will do everything they can to raise each competitor to the level of their potential. The rating systems in their sports will generally prove them right.

We can identify talent in almost every kind of endeavor, and we can establish performance rating systems, but no such system exists for politicians. We badly need one. Elections and reelections merely measure a candidate's ability to raise money and talk a good game. I could not find any rating systems for politicians. No system rates the performance of individuals or groups. Nothing can help voters make informed decisions based on comparisons. However, I did find some interesting data on citizen satisfaction in various countries around the world. The figures below represent the percentages of satisfied and dissatisfied citizens in select countries and groupings.[5] (These numbers differ slightly from those in Chapter 1 and come from another source, but the significance is the same.)

	Satisfied	Dissatisfied
Country Median	45%	51%
United States	40%	58%
Canada	61%	39%
Sweden	69%	30%
Germany	56%	43%
Russia	44%	49%

Note that we have the highest percentage of dissatisfied citizens. There are at least three possible explanations for these figures: (1) the expectations of U.S. citizens are too high, and our political system cannot live up to those expectations, while the citizens in Russia have low expectations, (2) the data from some countries is inaccurate, or (3) our political system is failing us.

The only meaningful means we have to measure customer (citizen) satisfaction shows us that more people are unhappy with our election results than are happy. We have three choices: lower our expectations, accept poor performance, or make changes.

Speaking of expectations, I earlier questioned whether we should tell grade schoolers they can be anything they want to be or whether we should be realistic and steer them toward a path that suits them and their potential. Physically, mentally, and psychologically, we all have strengths and weaknesses. People with greater knowledge should guide young people toward areas where their strengths will serve them well and away from areas that will most likely lead to disappointment. Along that line, I sometimes wish I had been guided into boxing when I was ten or eleven. In boxing, long arms are an asset, not a liability. I had good hand speed and big hands that make big fists. I had punching power, too. I didn't get into boxing until much later. Boxing classes were required for the first two semesters of our first year at West Point. I weighed about 150 pounds, so I was placed in the lightweight division. At the end of the first semester, I won the division. For kicks, the instructor had me box the winner of the heavyweight group. He weighed about 170 pounds. I beat him, too. The point is that we have the means to evaluate potential and rate performance. The two should agree, and we should put them to good use.

I started writing this book right after the assault on the Capitol on January 6, 2021. Donald Trump's second impeachment was starting. Shortly after, another event occurred that is representative of our political strife. On February 17, 2021, David Perdue, the former Georgia senator who lost reelection in a runoff in January, filed papers to run for the Senate seat held by Raphael Warnock in 2022.[6] Senator Warnock was just elected but was filling a seat vacated by Senator Johnny Isakson, so that seat will require a new election in two years. Senator Perdue was in office for six years. The fact that he could not win reelection in a state that has a long history of electing only Republican senators could be seen as a sign that he did not do what Georgia voters expected, yet he's already gearing up for a bid to return to the Senate. His thinking and his actions over the last six years deserve some attention.

The preliminaries for an election that is more than twenty months away are already starting. David Perdue can now aggressively chase the money he will need to pursue election. According to a statement he made upon filing, it is essential that Georgia win back the seat so the state will not have two "radical liberals" in the Senate. It is also important to give Republicans control of the Senate so that President Biden will have to deal with a "balanced government."[6] Why did David Perdue fail to mention all of the good things he has done for the state of Georgia during his six years in the Senate and all of the good things he plans to do if elected again? Instead, he wants to make sure that gridlock returns so that all of those allegedly radical Democrats cannot have their way. He has five million dollars left over from the previous campaign, and he'll have no trouble raising all he needs for another campaign that will last months. It will be another campaign where voters can learn every bad thing they ever wanted to know about the candidates.

The other senator from Georgia, Kelly Loeffler, was also defeated and also announced that she, too, would consider another run for the Senate. She, like Perdue, is an extreme conservative, and both lost to extremists from the Democratic Party. In a realistic prognosis of what will happen in Georgia, Loeffler and

Perdue will both pursue the Republican Party's endorsement to run for the Senate seat. Raphael Warnock will be the Democratic candidate. It makes no difference who wins between Perdue and Loeffler. The citizens of Georgia will again end up with a choice between the extreme left and the extreme right. The names might change but the game unfolds in the same way, and the outcome will be more of the same.

I asked why David Perdue did not remind us of the good things he did and what he planned to do that would make a strong case for his return to the Senate. Perhaps he didn't do anything of note, or perhaps he didn't think that the ability to get things done should matter. It seems that what is most important to David Perdue is to stop his opponents from getting things done, a good example of why we need a rating system for politicians.

If Georgia voters put Perdue back in the Senate in 2022 and Ossoff is the other senator from Georgia, the combination is likely to produce more conflict and little else.

West Point has a mission statement. I was on the team that wrote the mission statement for Allied Security. The preamble of our Constitution is a mission statement. I doubt that many politicians are aware of any mission other than that of their own selfish making. At every level of government, we need a mission statement to devise a way to rate performance with some level of relativity. Members of the Senate should have a mission statement that serves as a reference point for evaluating and rating performance. The rating could be done by peers or by voters using a concept I will present in a later chapter.

Dr. Deming is against slogans. I understand why. In the 1960s, the Army adopted a slogan. It was "Zero Defects." It didn't gain much traction. But I think there are meaningful slogans, such as "Duty-Honor-Country." If our public servants tried to live up to that motto, our political climate would be much more temperate.

Yes, my ideas might sound wild, but they are options, and wild options are permissible when brainstorming. We have great technology and expertise today that we could apply to the election problem. Someone or some group, using available technology, should be able to devise a way to rate politicians and help voters evaluate candidates based on past performance, the most meaningful indicator of future performance.

In 2017, C-SPAN had ninety-one historians rate forty-three presidents.[7] Each president was ranked one to ten in the following ten areas: public persuasion, crisis leadership, economic management, moral authority, international relations, administrative skills, relationship with Congress, vision/setting an agenda, pursuit of equal justice for all, and performance within the context of the times. After the scores were combined, the top seven were the same seven presidents I used in the chapter titled "Masters of Productivity," and I wrote that chapter *before* I saw the C-SPAN article published on February 15, 2021 in the *Atlanta Journal*.

Evaluating performance requires that you establish standards; otherwise, there is no relativity. Then you need to compare performance with those standards. If you can identify the top and the bottom performers, you can then take appropriate action.

Because many individuals and groups are uninformed or biased, you have to work at getting enough truthful information to rate those who are performing as public servants. Search for facts. Compare their performance to your expectations. Don't accept excuses. Discount attempts to redirect your examination to the shortcomings of the opposition. Focus on this question: "What has he done recently to make this country a better place to live?"

Selected Quotes on Character and Leadership

"Leadership is a potent combination of strategy and character. But if you must be without one,
be without the strategy."

"I admire men of character, and I judge character . . . mostly (by) how they deal with their subordinates."

"Going to war without France is like going hunting without an accordion."

–General Norman Schwarzkopf[8]

"Leadership is solving problems."

"I don't want to spend the rest of my life giving speeches."

"If you are going to achieve excellence in big things, you develop the habit in little matters. Excellence is . . . a prevailing attitude."

–Secretary of State Colin Powell[9]

"The first step of leadership is to be right with yourself. Integrity is the basis of leadership."

"You might not be able to control your circumstances, but you can control your response to your circumstances."

–Secretary of State Condoleezza Rice[10]

"Whatever the job you are asked to do at whatever level, do a good job, because your reputation is your résumé."

"I am a problem solver."

–Secretary of State Madeleine Albright[11]

"There are five elements of leadership: honor, confidence, competence, compassion, and humility."

–Medal of Honor Recipient Paul Bucha[12]

Chapter 9

Lawyers and Politics

"Lawyers spend their professional careers shoveling smoke." [1]

–Oliver Wendell Holmes

S ome unidentified force must pull lawyers into politics. An analysis done on the one hundred senators in office on February 15, 2021 showed that 45% studied law in college and 30% practiced law before entering the Senate. When you consider that there are at least ten other general areas of employment, such as business, education, health care, sports/entertainment, military service, clergy, and so on, that such a large percentage of politicians come out of the law profession is significant.

Does law training help make one more competent in the field of politics? Do lawyers tend to have the type of character that fits politics well?

Politics involves a great deal of conflict. When pursuing election, contenders for the same office verbally attack each other, and they don't always fight fair. If elected, they face even more conflict. Which came first, the lawyers or the acrimonious environment? Are lawyers attracted to politics because the environment is full of conflict and conflict suits their character, or have lawyers created and maintained a culture in politics that is a reflection of their personality? The answer doesn't matter. What is important is that the situation has become self-perpetuating. If we want to reduce conflict and gridlock in politics, we have to change the culture. We must modify the concept of what constitutes acceptable behavior and remove those who can't work as part of a team.

The evidence does not support the conclusion that lawyers are especially competent in politics. If they were, better than 50% of Americans would be happy with their government, and I would not be writing this book. Perhaps 150 years ago, lawyers were a good choice because they probably made up a higher percentage of Americans with good educations. Maybe their confrontational style was productive in those times. Things have changed.

Legal education and the experience of working as a lawyer do not appear to give attorneys an advantage in the area of competence. It might even be detrimental where character is concerned.

In an earlier chapter, we covered the DISC method of behavior analysis, the importance of values, and Maslow's Hierarchy of Needs. These personnel selection tools are useful when matching the character traits that will be most effective in a particular job. When the traits of the individual and those that are suitable for a position don't match, the performance, as measured by results, is usually unsatisfactory.

Even if evidence indicated that lawyers make good (i.e., productive) politicians, too much of a good thing might not always be beneficial. This idea is comparable to the CEO I mentioned who surrounded himself with others who, like himself, operated well in an unfriendly environment, but not as well in a friendly environment. The result was more conflict than teamwork. To have a more productive culture, a better mix of people in terms of education, work experience, and behavioral patterns is preferable.

As in any profession, some lawyers are competent and others are not. Some lawyers are ethical and others are not. In politics, competence matters, but so do teamwork and ethical conduct. We have a two-party system that could be construed as two teams, and neither team plays in a way that makes for a good game. If we compare it to a football game, it seems as if almost every play draws a flag, preventing anyone from scoring. The blame does not fall only on the lawyers, but their *modus operandi* seems to be carrying the day. Here are two interesting quotes from well-known lawyers:

"I love to argue. I've always loved to argue."[2]

—Supreme Court Justice Antonin Scalia

"When you have no basis for an argument,
abuse the plaintiff."[3]

—Marcus Cicero

Politicians are always debating ideas and methods. But they need not go at it with such zeal that agreement rarely happens. Unproductive debate happens more and more because our election system tends to put those in office who are at the extremes of the political spectrum and who excel at arguing. If we could put in place a system that allowed moderates to compete and succeed, the gap between ideals would narrow, and we would have a much better chance of making progress. Moderates should be a powerful force in our government because the majority of Americans are moderates, or would be if they weren't driven to extremes by the way our politicians play the game.

Of our seven top-ranked presidents, three were educated in law, two were from the military, one was from business, and one was a historian and author. Of the top two, one was from the military (George Washington) and the other was a lawyer (Abraham Lincoln). Both were dedicated to selfless service to the nation. Both had the exceptional ability to pull together a group of people and create a team that produced results. Their leadership skills were the quality that made them outstanding politicians. There is no proof that people with a law background have an edge in teamwork or leadership.

Some famous lawyers have made great comments about lawyers, politicians, politics, and governance. It is fascinating to see how little has changed in this regard over thousands of years. Lawyers have dominated politics for centuries, yet lawyers are critical of lawyers in general and lawyers in politics.

Marcus T. Cicero was a Roman statesman, lawyer, and scholar. He lived from 106 BC to 43 BC.[4] He died at the hands of Roman soldiers who were supporters of Mark Antony. They cut off Cicero's head. His words suggest that many things have not changed over the last two thousand years:[5]

"A nation can survive its fools, and even the ambitious. But it cannot survive treason from within. An enemy at the gates is less formidable, for he is known and carries his banner openly. But the traitor moves amongst those within the gate freely, his sly whispers rustling through all the alleys, heard in the very halls of government itself."

"Do not blame Caesar; blame the people of Rome who have so enthusiastically acclaimed and adored him and rejoiced in their loss of freedom and danced in his path and gave him triumphal processions. Blame the people who hail him when he speaks in the Forum of the 'new, wonderful good society' which shall now be Rome. Interpreted to mean 'more money, more ease, more security, more living fatly at the expense of the industrious.'"

"Six mistakes mankind keeps making century after century: believing that personal gain is made by crushing others; worrying about things that cannot be changed or corrected; insisting that a thing is impossible because we cannot accomplish it; refusing to set aside trivial preferences; neglecting development and refinement of the mind; attempting to compel others to believe and live as we do."

"Politicians are not born; they are excreted."

"When a government becomes powerful, it is destructive, extravagant, and violent; it is a usurer which takes bread from innocent mouths and deprives honorable men of their substance, for votes with which to perpetuate itself."

"Never was a government that was not composed of liars, malefactors, and thieves."

"If we are forced, at every hour, to watch or listen to horrible events, this constant stream of ghastly impressions will deprive even the most delicate among us of all respect for humanity."

"We learn nothing from history except that we learn nothing from history."

"The wise are instructed by reason, average minds by experience, the stupid by necessity, and the brute by instinct."

"There are two ways to resolve conflicts, through violence or through negotiation. Violence is for wild beasts; negotiation is for human beings."

"Any man can make mistakes, but only an idiot persists in his error."

Cicero articulated these ideas two thousand years ago, yet we have not made much progress. Many of these same thoughts apply as much today as they did to the Roman Empire. The last two quotes fit right in with the thinking of Deming. As Cicero implied, however, we should not give up, even if some things seem impossible. Later, I will list more quotes, moving from the distant past to the present. Many have said what I am trying to say, but they have done so with much greater elegance. Their reputations might make their comments more impressionable.

My own political ambitions ended when I was seventeen. Somehow, I was elected president of my senior class in high school. I quickly realized that it was a job I didn't want and that I should never get involved in politics again. Just as I had characteristics that prohibited me from being an elite gymnast, I had character flaws that prevented me from being a successful politician. The first ill-fitting characteristic is that I am introverted. If I have to reach the fifth floor of a building and six people are waiting for the elevator, I will happily take the stairs. My wife, an extreme extrovert, would take the elevator and make at least five new friends by the time she reached the fifth floor.

The second characteristic is that I like to get things done. No, that's not right; I absolutely have to get things done. There is a story about a lumberjack who was the best in his area with an ax. He made $20 an hour cutting logs with his ax. He could chop logs for eight hours a day. He was offered $100 an hour to "chop" on a log with a sledge hammer that was the same weight as his ax. He went at it for ten minutes and stopped. He said, "I can't do it; I have to see chips fly."

Every aspect of behavior falls on a continuum. On the continuum for "results orientation," I would be in the 99th percentile. I take ten minutes to walk fifty feet to the mailbox because I have to stop and pull weeds, collect dog droppings, or think about my next home improvement project. In today's political climate, I would last about ten minutes as a politician. If the environment were to somehow become ideal for true and productive governance, I might last a few days.

When interviewing prospects for a position, experienced screeners look for patterns of behavior. Those patterns are predictors of future behavior. I left the Army because I was not a good fit. I left P&G to work for a smaller company. I retired from Allied Security at fifty-one and started a small home-improvement company. The pattern should be clear. For me, big is bad, and small is good. Last summer, I cut down a cherry tree and made three end tables from the wood. I like to work with my mind and my hands. I, too, need to see the chips fly. I will happily spend four hours pulling out a tree stump. Put me in a meeting for four hours, and I will be pulling out my hair.

Thankfully, others have a high level of results orientation, and they thrive in big organizations. The right system will match the right people with the right job.

The last characteristic is a little embarrassing. I might have been a good little thief, but I was a bad little fibber. I learned from experience.

We lived in a development with community swimming pools that all residents could use. I was nine and had a ten-year-old brother. We were eleven months apart. To get into the pool without a parent, you had to be ten. I convinced my mother, who was ill at the time, that it would be okay if just my brother and I went. When we reached the entrance, my brother went in first without any questions. I came to the gate, and a nice woman asked how old I was. I answered, "Ten." She looked at my brother and asked if we were twins. I said, "No." She then asked how many months we were apart. I knew the honest answer was eleven, but since I had already lied about being ten, I said we were three months apart. Somehow she knew I was lying. At the time, I was sure it was something in my voice. Years later, I learned my mistake. I hadn't made good eye contact. Nonetheless, my mother was not happy when she had to come to the pool and get me. I took the experience to heart and decided I'd better avoid jobs that required the modification of facts.

Gaius Sallust Crispus was a statesman in Rome during the same period as Cicero but lived a little longer, dying in 34 BC. He made the following statements:[6]

"Harmony makes small things grow;
lack of it makes great things decay."

"To someone searching for power,
the poorest man is the most useful."

"There were few who preferred honor to money."

"Every bad precedent originated as a justified measure."

Clarence Darrow, a famous lawyer, said,

"The trouble with law is lawyers." [7]

Chief Justice of the Supreme Court Earl Warren said the following:[8]

"To get what you want, stop doing what isn't working."

"A republic is not an easy form of government to live under, and when the responsibility of citizenship is evaded, democracy decays and authoritarianism takes over."

Barbara Jordan, a politician from Texas, lived from 1936 to 1996 and had many insightful things to say, including the following:[9]

"It is reason, and not passion, which must guide our deliberations, guide our debate, guide our decision."

"What the people want is very simple—they want an America as good as its promise."

"The citizens of America expect more. They deserve and they want more than a recital of problems."

"If we promise as public officials, we must deliver. If we as public officials propose, we must produce."

"This is the great danger America faces. That we will cease to be one nation and become instead a collection of interest groups: city against suburb, region against region, individual against individual, each seeking to satisfy private wants."

"We cannot improve on the system of government handed down to us by the founders of the Republic. There is no way to improve upon that. But what we can do is find new ways to implement that system and realize our destiny."

Jordan hit every nail squarely on the head. Politics involves too much passion and not enough reason and drive to give citizens what they want and deserve. Officials have to stop making empty promises. She clearly saw in our future the divisive condition we have reached. She rightfully placed the blame on those wanting only to satisfy their private wants. The basic principles of our Constitution are sound. The mission is still appropriate. As she stated, it does not prohibit us from finding new and better ways to make the system work.

I touched on my short-lived career in politics. I also gave serious thought to becoming a lawyer. As an Army officer, you get involved in military law. Our armed forces have their own criminal justice system spelled out in the Uniform Code of Military Justice. Young officers participate in the defense and prosecution of service personnel accused of minor crimes such as sleeping on guard duty. As officers advance in rank, they participate on court martial boards where the crimes are more serious. They can be a juror or a judge depending on their rank and the type of crime. I found it fascinating. I could also see how easy it was to get caught up in trying to win an argument and lose sight of everything else. I took the law school aptitude test and received a high enough grade to get into a good law school, but I could not handle the costs of school at the time, so I went to work for P&G.

At P&G, I got involved with the law to some extent because of my work in the security group. My real involvement, however, came with my work with Allied Security. As the senior manager for both operations and personnel, I had to handle complaints involving discrimination by employees. With more than seven thousand employees across the country, we had our share of such claims. In the twenty years I was engaged in these cases, we had about one hundred claims. About ninety of those were resolved easily. Many were closed before a lawyer got involved. Eight of the ten remaining claims were problematic, and lawyers from both sides were involved. We settled those eight, but always at a cost. Two cases could not be closed and were scheduled for trial.

In one case set for trial, we requested the judge grant us a summary judgment. Our attorney sent a detailed summary of the case to the judge stating all of the reasons why the case should be dismissed without going to trial. It is unusual for a judge to dismiss a case because the prevailing thinking is that people deserve their day in court. The judge wrote a scathing opinion that granted us summary judgment and took the plaintiff and his attorney to task. It cost us only about $75,000.

In the second case, the claim went to trial. The plaintiff believed her case was rock solid, as did her attorney. The jury trial lasted almost a week. After closing arguments, the jury returned a verdict in about one hour. The jurors had lunch during that time, too. The verdict was in our favor. The plaintiff and the attorney got nothing. We received a legal bill for about $150,000.

A book cannot have a chapter titled "Lawyers and Politics" without having at least one joke about lawyers. There is one below, and others appear at the end of this chapter where you'll also find some great quotes about politics. The joke is one I wrote, and as you read the joke, think about the $75,000 and the $150,000 it cost us to close two cases that did not settle.

> A mobster dies and finds himself at the pearly gates of heaven talking to Saint Peter.
>
> **Mobster:** "This must be some kind of mistake. I made my living for thirty years running an extortion racket. I thought for sure I would go to hell. I don't know how many times I told businessmen that I would burn their building down if they didn't pay up."
>
> **Saint Peter:** "Hell has a daily quota, and you had a lucky day. A lot of lawyers died today, and hell had no more room. As far as extortionists go, you're small potatoes compared to many lawyers. They're always telling businessmen that if they don't settle, they'll sue."

I have heard the threat of a legal suit many times. The joke isn't all that funny, but neither is getting threatened and knowing you are going to lose money no matter what happens. The minimum amount to settle was never less than $10,000. Lawyers knew $10,000 was less than the cost of continuing the legal process.

I cannot close this subject without telling my favorite story about lawyers. We were facing an employment practices violation that really troubled me. We were threatened with a suit because we fired a national guardsman after he returned from emergency duty in the wake of an earthquake. The details are complicated. Both sides had confidence in their case.

I flew to Los Angles with my attorney for the taking of depositions. Their side presented their proof. It was our branch manager's college yearbook. It was opened to a picture of her at a protest against the Vietnam War. They were convinced that the image proved she was anti-military and explained why she had fired the guardsman. I will always remember their smug faces.

I then asked, "Where is my yearbook?" I got strange looks. I explained that our management team had seen this termination as problematic and that they had come to me as the head of Human Resources. I had reviewed the entire case and personally made the decision to terminate the man. The branch manager had played a very minor role in the decision, and I had played the major role. What they needed was *my* yearbook for the year 1965 from West Point. The smug faces were gone.

I stood and announced, "We are done here." My attorney tried but was unable to stop me from walking out of the room. He kept telling me that I was making a mistake. We soon received a letter from their side offering to settle for the standard fee of $10,000.

Lawyers have been heavily involved in politics for thousands of years. They created the rules for the game. They brought them from the courtroom, along with the manners and divisive conduct permissible in court. The two-party system acts as a catalyst that makes an inherently divisive culture even more toxic. People from all walks of life go into politics but not people of all types of behavioral patterns. Many people with behavioral patterns and skills that would make them great leaders and problem solvers are completely turned off by the culture of politics.

In the last five years, I have paid particular attention to three people who went directly from the business world to public office at the federal level. One was Donald Trump, and the other two were senators from Georgia: David Perdue and Kelly Loeffler. All three used their business success and the fact that they were not politicians as part of their campaign message. It sounded good to me, but it didn't turn out well. It ended badly for two reasons.

First, they were not politicians before taking office, but their personalities allowed them to adjust quickly to the culture. Second, as W. Edwards Deming stated, "Put a good person in a bad system, and the bad system wins, no contest." [10]

Our political culture is one of confrontation. It is consistent with a long history that has not been productive nor changed in any direction toward greater productivity from one century to the next. If we expect our future to be different from the past, we need to consider changes. The culture we have in place is fed and perpetuated by an election system that mirrors that culture. It is hostile and divisive. The winners gain victory by compromising themselves, and many losers become embittered. Politics and elections can and should be more like a game of football. The players should respect one another and play hard but fair.

———

Lawyers have been and can continue to be great politicians, but they need to discard the culture and antics of the courtroom. The election system needs to change accordingly and attract people who are suited for getting things done through teamwork. Teamwork is the key to positive productivity.

As a voter, don't automatically think that lawyers make better lawmakers. The difficult part of governing is deciding what needs to be done to help the majority of the people and then accomplishing those goals through leadership, teamwork, and consensus building. Great politicians are great at identifying and solving problems. They need not be experts in the law.

Lawyer Jokes[11]

"What's the difference between a lawyer and a boxing referee? A boxing referee doesn't get paid more for a long fight."

"How many lawyer jokes are there? Only three; the rest are true stories."

"What do you throw a drowning lawyer? His partners."

"What's the difference between a lawyer and a leech? After you die, a leech stops sucking your blood."

"What do you call a lawyer with an IQ of fifty? Senator."

"What do you call a lawyer with an IQ of one hundred? Your Honor."

"How many lawyers does it take to screw in a lightbulb? Three. One to climb the ladder. One to shake it. And one to sue the ladder company."

"How does an attorney sleep? First, he lies on one side; then, he lies on the other."

"What are lawyers good for? They make used car salesmen look good."

"What's the difference between an accountant and a lawyer? Accountants know they're boring."

"What do you call a smiling, nice person at a bar association convention? The caterer."

Quotes about Politics[12]

"Take our politicians: they're a bunch of yo-yos. The presidency is now a cross between a popularity contest and a high-school debate."

–Saul Bellow

"Politicians and corporations have always placed economic interests above moral interests."

–Marianne Thieme

"In order to become the master, the politician poses as the servant."

–Charles de Gaulle

"Under democracy, one party always devotes its chief energies to trying to prove that the other party is unfit to rule—and both commonly succeed, and are right."

–H. L. Mencken

"Mothers all want their sons to grow up to be president, but they don't want them to become politicians in the process."

–John F. Kennedy

Chapter 10

Change and the Constitution

"We the people are the rightful masters of both Congress and the courts, not to overthrow the Constitution but to overthrow the men who pervert the Constitution." [1]

–Abraham Lincoln

This book is about change. Change is good and necessary. This chapter probes questions related to change and the Constitution. What is the process for changing the Constitution? How many meaningful changes have been made to the Constitution since it was written in 1787? What changes have been advocated by Constitutional scholars in the recent past? How else can we make good changes to our system of governance without making changes to the Constitution? Do we really need to make changes? Finally, if we initiated a brainstorming session that invited any and all options for changing the Constitution for consideration, what might be some of the most extreme options?

On November 19, 1863, a gathering took place at a cemetery in

Gettysburg, Pennsylvania, to honor those who had died at the Battle of Gettysburg, which was fought from July 1 to July 3 of that year.[2] The primary speaker was a well-known orator, Edward Everett.[3] As was common at the time, he spoke for two hours. The next speaker was President Abraham Lincoln. He spoke just 272 words. After the president spoke, Everett told him, "I wish that I could flatter myself that I had come as near to the central idea of the occasion in two hours as you did in two minutes."[4] The Gettysburg Address is at the end of this chapter. It is recognized as one of the finest speeches ever made.

Consider the times and the timing. The battle ended one day shy of the eighty-seventh anniversary of the signing of the Declaration of Independence in 1776. The Union was, in fact, broken. Eleven states had seceded from the Union, forming the Confederate States of America, and had their own army, flag, currency, and president. The United States were no longer united, and we remained divided until the North won the war in 1865. Our history demonstrates how fragile democracy can be and how divisiveness can result in what most Americans think and hope is impossible.

The Civil War was the only major war ever fought on American soil. Deadly and destructive, it killed about 620,000 Americans, about 2% of the population.[5] In World War II, we lost 419,400, only 0.3% of the population.[6] The Civil War took from us one of the two best presidents ever to serve and replaced him with one of the worst. More than 150 years have elapsed since the Civil War ended, yet we still suffer the consequences. As evidence, some of the rioters who assaulted the Capitol on January 6, 2021 thought it appropriate to carry the flag of the Confederate States of America.

The Gettysburg Address features a masterful choice of words. It presents a message of poetic beauty, but the message itself, in its brevity, is even more important. Consider the final sentence:

"... that this nation, under God, shall have a new birth of freedom—and that *government of the people, by the people, for the people, shall not perish from the earth.*"

Our Constitution is also a brief document, considering that it establishes the manner in which our federal government operates. Brilliantly conceived at the time, it has served us well. The writers were wise enough to realize that circumstances would change and that the Constitution would need to change accordingly. As we explore changes in governance, we need to do so within the parameters set forth in the Constitution. We need to pay particular attention to what we can accomplish through changes in traditions and laws that are not part of the Constitution. Most importantly, we must keep the ultimate objective in mind, as Abraham Lincoln stated beautifully in his Gettysburg Address.

We came close to losing our Union 150 years ago. We need to act soon and wisely to prevent a repeat. If our Union splits again, we might not be as fortunate to have a leader like Lincoln in the White House. Regardless of who is in the White House, the price would be dear.

The Constitution refers to changes as *amendments*. Adding an amendment to the Constitution is a two-step process. The proposal, the first step, can be accomplished in two ways. One way is for the Senate and the House of Representatives, the two chambers of Congress, to get two-thirds of their members to agree to propose the amendment. The second way is for two-thirds of the state legislatures or conventions in the states to make the proposal. In either case, the second step, ratification—having it officially added to the Constitution—requires that three-fourths of the state legislatures or state conventions vote for it. There are twenty-seven amendments to the Constitution, but the first ten were added to the original Constitution at the time it was written.

Why was the content of the ten amendments not part of the basic document? The answer will make more sense if we have a better understanding of what was happening in 1787.

The manner of governance of the thirteen states was spelled out in the Articles of Confederation. Delegates from the thirteen states were invited to come to Philadelphia in May 1787 to revise the Articles of Confederation. Twelve states chose to send delegates. Rhode Island was not represented.[7] The number of delegates from each state varied from one to eight, with a total of fifty-five delegates. They started meeting on May 25. George Washington, a delegate from Virginia, was chosen to be the president of the convention.[7] Within a few days, the delegates decided to abandon the Articles of Confederation and start anew. The men had strong feelings about the outcome they wanted for the state they represented and the kind of federal government they wanted. At one extreme were those who wanted a powerful federal government, and at the other, those who wanted most of the power to govern at the state level. After a great deal of debate and many compromises over eighty-nine days of meetings from May to September,[8] one of the sticking points was whether there should be a listing of rights in the Constitution. With many delegates facing exhaustion from the long process, they finally resolved the issue by including a list of rights as the first ten amendments. Once the Constitution was drafted, it had to be ratified by nine of the thirteen states. That process took until June 1788.[9] The Constitutional Convention demonstrated that democracy is not easy, but with hard work and compromise, the people can achieve great things.

A review of the seventeen amendments added between 1795, when the eleventh amendment was ratified, and 1992, when the twenty-seventh amendment was ratified, reveals how few changes of consequence have taken place. I will review them by their impact on the mechanics of governance, from least to greatest.

Amendments eighteen and twenty-one, Prohibition and the Repeal of Prohibition, nullify each other, so they have no impact. Even if Prohibition had remained the law of the land, it had nothing to do with governance.

Amendments fifteen, nineteen, twenty-three, and twenty-six granted the right to vote to minorities, women, citizens of Washington D.C., and citizens at least eighteen years old, respectively. These additions were important to the voter base and critical steps toward equality. However, they did not change the mechanics of government.

Amendments thirteen and twenty-four abolished reprehensible conduct—slavery—and removed poll taxes so that all citizens could vote, but neither changed the way the federal government conducts business.

Amendment twenty-seven prevented representatives in Congress from granting themselves a pay increase during their two-year term of office. It would be interesting to do a cost/benefit analysis of this change. If it saved a lot of money, it would not reflect well on the character of those in Congress. Perhaps it was meant to be symbolic. Nevertheless, it had no impact on governance.

Another change that could be considered a "housekeeping" matter is more interesting because it is one of the few times that a change reflected the impact of new technology. All of the amendments covered so far are indicative of changes in attitude or the correction of minor flaws. Amendment twenty changed the dates of the presidential inauguration and the opening of Congress. The inauguration of George Washington took place on April 30, 1789.[10] The effective date of the Constitution was March 4, 1789. For the next 144 years, inaugurations were on March 4 unless that date fell on a Sunday. The four-month period from election day to

March 4 was needed to count the votes and get the new administration up and running. A four-month lag in the transition was both unnecessary and undesirable by 1933, but the change did not have much impact on the mechanics of the federal government.

The next five amendments are clarifications or additions. Up until World War II, every president had followed the tradition of holding office for only two terms. Franklin D. Roosevelt chose to disregard that tradition in 1940 when he ran and won reelection for a third term. The Depression and the country's precarious position with another war on the horizon influenced his decision to run and the voters' decision to keep him in office. In 1944, still in the midst of the war, he ran and won again, but he died in office soon after his fourth inauguration. Americans decided that the two-term limit was a good idea, and the twenty-second amendment made it law. It, too, changed little.

The federal government obtained the right to tax income with the sixteenth amendment in 1913. It was not the first time the federal government had implemented an income tax. Income taxes were in effect from 1861 until 1872.[11] Another attempt was made in 1894, but the Supreme Court resisted. For most of our history prior to 1913, income for the federal government was derived from tariffs. To avoid any further involvement of the Supreme Court, Congress proposed the sixteenth amendment in 1909. The states ratified it in 1913. By that time, some states were establishing their own income taxes. Wisconsin's income tax went into effect in 1912.[12] This amendment only gave the federal government another source of revenue, one that now requires a huge bureaucracy to operate, but it changed nothing else.

The last three amendments in this category of clarifications or additions are eleven, fourteen, and twenty-five. The eleventh amendment came about in 1795 when a citizen of South Carolina sued the State of Georgia. The Supreme Court ruled it was permissible, but Congress thought it was clearly prohibited by Article III, Section 2.[13] With ratification of the eleventh amendment, Congress clarified that such a lawsuit was not allowed. Amendment fourteen, along with the already mentioned thirteenth and fifteenth amendments, were Civil War-era laws to clarify the rights of former slaves and all races. The twenty-fifth amendment was an addition to establish a more comprehensive succession process for the president and vice president and define in greater detail how to deal with disabled officeholders. It followed in the wake of the assassination of President John F. Kennedy in 1963.[14] All five of these amendments served an important purpose but did not alter governance in any significant way.

The last two amendments to cover are twelve and seventeen. Even the two most impactful amendments had only minimal effect on governance. Amendment twelve was ratified in 1804. It resulted from the realization that having the vice president determined by the votes cast for president, with the president being the highest vote recipient and the vice president being the second highest vote recipient, was not working. Since 1804, each candidate for president has picked a partner to be the candidate for vice president. They run as a team. Amendment seventeen changed the way senators are elected. Until 1913, when amendment seventeen was ratified, state legislatures selected senators. Now, the voters in their states elect them. This change brought primaries into the picture. Some argue that nothing good has come from that change.

A closer look at the history of the seventeenth amendment is appropriate because it deals with the election of senators. More than one hundred years of debate passed, as well as several attempts to enact the seventeenth amendment, before actual ratification. Two problems brought about the change. One was the fear that senators were "buying" their positions from corrupt legislators. There might have been some truth to that concern. The second problem was deadlock. Legislatures could not always agree on who should fill the seats in the Senate, so the seats remained vacant for extended periods of time. In one case, a seat was open for two years.[15] This situation shows how difficult democracy can be and demonstrates how corruption produces failure in any system.

Little has changed since we moved from selection by legislatures to selection by voters. Money might have played a role in the original system, but it still plays a huge role. The difference is how it passes from those with the money to those who control selection.

To bring some relativity to this discussion and demonstrate why I have stated that the amendments individually and collectively have had little impact on governance, I will outline the thoughts of three different people on the changes that we should consider making to the Constitution. Two are authors of books on governance. I am the third. We are not alone in our thinking. If you go online, you will find hundreds of articles about changing the Constitution. Many point out, as I have throughout this book, that we have been too reluctant to make changes.

In his 2007 book, *A More Perfect Constitution*, Larry J. Sabato made twenty-three proposals to revitalize the Constitution.[16] I will list a few of his proposals that I consider meaningful changes in governance. I support some but not all of these proposals. I support the ones that represent changes that have the potential to solve some of our problems.

Sabato recommends term limits in Congress. He used a great quote from Richard Davies: "Politicians in government should be changed regularly, like diapers, and for the same reason."[17]

Five of his other proposals include the following:

1. Give the ten most populous states two additional senators and the next fifteen most populous one extra senator.

2. Presidents should serve for one six-year term.

3. Supreme Court justices should serve one fifteen-year term.

4. All able-bodied Americans should be required to serve their country for two years.

5. Appoint all former presidents and vice presidents to a new office of national senators.

Of Sabato's recommendations listed above, I strongly agree with his call for national service. I have an idea similar to his idea of national senators, but I don't think we need more senators as he suggests. I think we need "senior senators." I agree with his suggestion of term limits, but I want to connect it to performance and tie it into my idea of senior senators, an idea I explain in the last chapter.

Neal Simon's 2020 book, *Contract to Unite America*, offers some similar reforms.[18] He supports term limits. His other nine reforms deal with correcting problems in the election system and reducing conflict. His idea to adopt "ranked-choice-voting" is especially important.[19] However, his ideas for the election system are patches. As an example, he recommends cleaning up the debates, which are rituals in our current system.[20] I propose we eliminate them.

I would add two suggestions: create a powerful Federal Election Committee and an easier process for proposing and ratifying amendments. Chapter 13 covers these ideas, along with my suggestions for senior senators and term limits tied to performance.

Much of what happens in the American political arena is based on tradition and state or federal laws written to try to correct the undesirable consequences of those traditions. One example is traditions that have led to a governance system dominated by two parties.

The Constitution does not mention political parties, but they have evolved, as have state laws establishing primary elections to give voters some say in who the candidate will be for each party. The result is a dysfunctional subsystem within the larger dysfunctional election system. It is part of the reason we often end up with extremists to choose between at election time. Another example is the extensive use of TV and other forms of media to flood voters with candidate exposure. The costs of such long-running extravaganzas can be billions of dollars, so we have laws to control how the candidates obtain and use this money. As fast as lawmakers can patch a loophole in those financing laws, clever campaign managers find new loopholes. These two traditions need to be replaced.

————

We have reached the point when we have to face reality and come to the only sensible conclusion: we have to make meaningful changes to our system of governance. Tinkering and patching will not get the job done.

Changing traditions and laws might be a good starting point, but the result will not be sufficient in the long run. The Constitution was designed for change, and we should not be reluctant to make changes that would clearly improve our system of governance.

Our current situation is not due to a flaw in one element of our governance system. It's not the people. It's not the processes. It's not the technologies. It's a system-wide problem. As a voter, pay attention to those politicians who are different. They are the ones who say we must change what we are doing. Dismiss those who tell you that the solution to make everything better is to replace the opposition. We have waited long enough for that solution to work. I'll close this chapter with the quote by W. Edwards Deming that started this book:

"It is not necessary to change.
Survival is not mandatory."[21]

Address Delivered at the Dedication of the Cemetery at Gettysburg

Abraham Lincoln
November 19, 1863

Four score and seven years ago, our fathers brought forth on this continent, a new nation, conceived in Liberty, and dedicated to the proposition that all men are created equal.

Now we are engaged in a great civil war, testing whether that nation, or any nation so conceived and dedicated, can long endure. We are met on a great battle-field of that war. We have come to dedicate a portion of that field, as a final resting place for those who here gave their lives that that nation might live. It is altogether fitting and proper that we should do this.

But, in a larger sense, we cannot dedicate—we cannot consecrate—we cannot hallow—this ground. The brave men, living and dead, who struggled here, have consecrated it, far above our poor power to add or detract. The world will little note, nor long remember what we say here, but it can never forget what they did here. It is for us the living, rather, to be dedicated here to the unfinished work which they who fought here have thus far so nobly advanced. It is rather for us to be here dedicated to the great task remaining before us— that from these honored dead we take increased devotion to that cause for which they gave the last full measure of devotion—that we here highly resolve that these dead shall not have died in vain—that this nation, under God, shall have a new birth of freedom—and that government of the people, by the people, for the people, shall not perish from the earth.

Chapter 11

Problem Solving 101

"Think logically, and you have a chance to solve a problem.
Reacting emotionally to it prolongs and worsens
your dilemma." [1]

–Steward Stafford

P roblem solving and getting things done are almost the same. I will outline a general step-by-step procedure for solving problems. I will focus on a universal method, creating the most conducive culture, getting the most out of the people involved, and the many tools and techniques that are available.

I'll set the stage with a quote *and* a joke. Haresh Sippy said, "To crack a serious problem, crack a joke."[1] The joke is a one-liner from George Carlin, "I put a dollar in a change machine. Nothing changed."[2] The quote implies that a problem has a solution and that humor is a good way to start finding one. The joke contains a lesson about solving problems. Throwing money at a problem usually does nothing more than give you more of what you had. Money only produces a good change if it makes a bad system better.

Problem solving can be enhanced by study and improved by practice. The word "problem" has a negative connotation, but it need not be the case. Problem solving can be an enjoyable adventure, such as buying a new house or developing a plan for your two children to become better tennis players. I'll provide sufficient material to show how to improve problem-solving skills and perhaps whet appetites for studying the subject further.

Many great quotes refer to the subject of problem solving. I have selected some valuable ones and included them at the end this chapter.

Each of us face minor problems day after day. Periodically, we must deal with major problems. A minor problem might be something as routine as getting the car in for an oil change. A larger problem might be fulfilling your life's dream of watching a baseball game in every major-league ballpark around the country. The material in this chapter is applicable to these types of problems. However, my target, rather than the various problems that individuals face, is the type of problem thrown at a group of people. We can learn much more from situations in which a diverse group of people, such as a team in the workplace, must solve a problem or in which citizens are organizing some type of civics project. Problem solving in these situations requires a better understanding of how to get the right people on the team, how to create a positive culture, and how to maximize the contributions of each team member.

Sometimes the easiest way to get something done is to do it yourself, but that approach might not produce the best result. Frequently, this method also results in a solution rejected by those who experience the impact because they had no opportunity to participate. We have discussed the concepts of TQM in the context of problem solving, and TQM is known as Democracy in Industry.

Chapters 1 and 2 presented the first two steps in problem solving: problem recognition and problem definition. In some instances, we might recognize two or more problems within the same environment at the same time. If resources are insufficient to handle all of the problems at once, people must decide the order in which the problems need addressing. This decision could be perceived as another step in the method or as part of the first step.

For our purposes, we will assume that a problem has been recognized and determined to be worthy of a team effort. In some cases, the group that recognizes the problem and assigns it for solution is not the same group that will do the actual problem solving. There are also instances in which problem solving is the day-to-day assignment of a team. It is just another term for getting things done.

Consider a team that is responsible for putting refrigerators on the sales floor of appliance stores around the country. Each model has to be competitive and profitable. The team will produce one model, and as soon as it is finished, it will review that product's success and how the team can improve the next model. The situation might be that the team sees five things that would please customers but can only implement three before the next model has to hit the showroom floor. The team figures out how to do those three things and sees the results of those changes as it starts on the next model. This scenario shows continuous improvement in action.

W. Edwards Deming graphically presented the concept in a PDCA Cycle:[3]

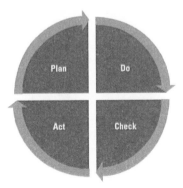

PDCA stands for Plan, Do, Check, and Act. The end of this chapter features full explanations of the four parts of the cycle.

Earlier, I said problem-solving and getting things done are almost the same. I make a small distinction between the two. I use a TQM system to get things done. Whenever there is a task before me, I systematically look at three elements: people, technology, and process. While applying the system, I consider the environment, including the time and money available. For each step in the problem-solving method, I employ that "getting-things-done" system to work through that step. It is especially helpful when brainstorming options and evaluating those options.

Here is a real example of using the getting-things-done system in problem recognition. I received a letter from our natural gas provider that reminded me that I am responsible for checking for leaks in the line from the main line to our swimming pool heater. I could assume that we didn't have a leak or test to see whether we did. Being a pessimist, and introverts are frequently pessimists, too, I elected to check the line.

Conditions: The line was above ground and only about twenty feet long. I had some leak-detection fluid on hand. I had time to spare.

People: I could do the work or hire a heating and air conditioning contractor who would know what to do and have the equipment to do the job. I chose to do it myself.

Technology: I considered three types of technology. I could use my nose, which is free. I could use leak-detection fluid, which costs under $10. I could buy a gas-detection meter for about $100. Each option had pros and cons. My nose was cheap but not foolproof. The meter was effective and could be used again, but I would have to go the store and pay $100. I already had some leftover fluid, so I decided to use it.

Process: I could have used any number of processes: pour it on, use a spray bottle, or brush it on.

I went into great detail to demonstrate the entire approach to a simple issue, but the same approach applies to any problem. In this example, I methodically worked through the steps to see whether I had a leak (a problem). If I had found a leak, I would have then used the same steps to determine how to fix the leak.

The importance of problem definition, the second step in the methodology, cannot be emphasized enough. Einstein made the point well: "If I had an hour to solve a problem, I'd spend fifty-five minutes thinking about the problem and five minutes thinking about the solution."[4]

By popular request from readers of the draft manuscript, I am returning to the "Little-Thief" story. I added more complexity and lessons. The new situation is the following. I am now Ken, the dad, and the little thief is my son Kenny. Ken is no longer a tavern owner; he is a licensed private investigator.

I have determined that quarters are disappearing from the piggy bank. I have a problem and consider my options. Remember that I am a licensed private investigator, have access to surveillance equipment, and know how to use it. I have interviewed many people suspected of wrong-doing.

I spend considerable time thinking about the problem. I decide that I can't make it go away by getting rid of the bank. One person of interest is Tilly, the housekeeper. It can't be Tilly. Her fingers are too thick. The most likely thief is Kenny. He's the smallest and the most materialistic. Flying model airplanes is an expensive hobby for a kid. I'll start with Kenny.

I could setup my surveillance equipment, or I could use my interviewing skills. I select the latter. I carefully plan everything: where the interview will take place, how I will look, and what I will say. I've spent lots of time thinking about the problem. I love my son, but if he is stealing, I have to correct his behavior. I am not a fan of corporal punishment, and there will be none in this instance. I think showing Kenny that there are consequences for improper conduct is important, and it is my duty as a dad. I actually feel sorry for him. I can easily see myself in his position.

I sit behind my big desk in my home office. I have Tilly come in and ask her to bring Kenny to me. As she leaves, I ask her to close the door. Kenny knocks and enters. He immediately sees that I have my "serious-dad" face on. I tell him to sit in the big chair in front of my desk. On the desk is my surveillance equipment. I say, "I think you know why you're here. Do you want to tell me about it? And before you speak, realize that if you lie, I'll know and you will be in twice as much trouble."

It's over. Kenny will do one or more of three things, and they all involve bodily fluids. He will cry, sweat, or pee. Detectives call this a "tell." The truth come outs. Kenny will be punished, and he will pay back what he stole. I take no joy in this entire situation; but, of my options, I thought it produced an acceptable outcome. Part of Kenny's lesson is experiencing apprehension and discomfort to an extent that will deter him from stealing again. Maybe Kenny will even mature into an adult of good character.

Note that in the system, process is important. The technology includes not only the surveillance equipment but also the entire setting. Tilly plays an important role. I want Kenny on edge even before he enters my office. I want him to have to knock on the door. I put the little thief out of business by using a methodical problem-solving system.

For larger problems, after problem recognition and selection, a team of people need to tackle the issue. The general nature of the problem will help determine the size of the team and its makeup. For most problems, a group of five to ten is good. The more areas of specialized knowledge that the problem touches on, the more people you might need. You might even need teams within the team that focus on a specific aspect of the problem.

Nothing good will get done until the team comes up with an in-depth understanding and *written* definition of the problem. The definition should be written because it takes more understanding to state an issue concisely in writing than to say it. Writing it also helps ensure that everyone is working on the same problem and that it undergoes redefinition only for a good reason and with all players involved. Understanding a problem requires research, data collection, and data analysis to determine relativity and establish standards for measuring performance. The effort of preparing this definition continues until the members agree that they have uncovered the root causes of the problem. They can then examine the options to address the problem.

Picking members for the team is similar to "hiring" people. We want people with several traits in common: they want to be involved, they know how to work with others and enjoy working with others, they are creative, they will respectfully say what is on their mind, and the reward they crave the most is to do great work. For many reasons, you also want people who are different. Some need to be introspective and pessimistic while others need to be extroverted and optimistic. Some should be methodical thinkers, and some should rely on intuition. You need some who can work on the details endlessly and some who are better at seeing the big picture. You also want people with different backgrounds, skills, and interests. These differences help the group look at a problem from all angles and come up with the widest possible range of options.

Several specific types of backgrounds are always advantageous. People with high-tech experience are invaluable. They often are familiar with technology that applies to the problem or know whether some technology could be adapted or created to be part of the solution. At least one should be an engineer. Engineers are systems-oriented thinkers and love to do the impossible. A good mathematician can help with data collection and analysis. Historians are great at research; they know what's been tried and how it worked, and they are good writers. On any gigantic problem, such as developing a better election system, I would include a world-class athlete. I have someone like Roger Staubach in mind. He graduated from a well-respected school, Annapolis, served in the Navy, was a superstar in a team sport, and became a successful real estate developer. Most accomplished athletes are masters at problem solving, and Staubach is one who has done it with class. Career military people make good team members, too. They know how to lead but have spent most of their careers as followers, so they can do either. The right mix of talent is key to producing the best possible result.

In some instances, you want an extraordinarily bright team member who is ignorant in the field of the problem. Here's an example from my own experience. I bought a light fixture that required assembly and installation. The instructions were obviously written by an engineer too knowledgeable about the light. He could not look at the installation as a novice homeowner would. The engineer considered some steps obvious that were not obvious to the average homeowner. A bright but uninformed technical writer could have written instructions that didn't require an engineering degree to understand and follow.

The team leader must be someone of broad competence and exemplary character. This person should be comfortable delegating and able to inspire individual and collective effort. The best leaders in this setting do not give orders. They divide the work in the best possible way, bring in resources the team needs, and coordinate the interaction among players as is necessary to keep the project moving toward the goal. Their role is to free the team members up to do what they do best. The leader shields the team from outsiders who want to influence the team, inadvertently slow down the team's progress, or worse, demoralize team members.

While the team leader controls the conduct of the individuals, the leader is also responsible for establishing the culture of the group. Negative and defeatist attitudes have no place in the culture. Difficulties should be open topics for discussion and treated as nothing but another obstacle to overcome. The fact that the solution may require new technology and a new process should make it more exciting. If the solution breaks with tradition or upsets some people, those issues are additional parts of the challenge. No member of the team should ever say, "That's not my problem." Every problem is part of the team's problem. Each member should welcome the chance to assist a teammate. There are no dumb questions and no dumb ideas. The team is a group of equals who must feel free to challenge anything they choose and have every idea they come up with given respectful consideration. A member might present an idea that is truly "dumb," but if team members are humiliated or embarrassed, they might not voice the next idea that comes to mind, an idea that could be brilliant. A team working together is democracy at work.

Once a team takes shape and the culture is off to a good start, the members use specialized tools and techniques to find the causes of the problem and define the problem. There are too many tools to list. I will cover two to give you a sample of the science involved.

Vilfredo Pareto, an economist, mathematician, and sociologist, was born in Paris, France in 1848 but spent most of his life in Italy and Switzerland. Well known in the field of problem solving, we have a chart that bears his name—The Pareto Chart.[4] He developed an interesting, but much criticized, theory on the distribution of objects and events. His theory is that for some unknown reason, many things have a predictable distribution—the ratio of 80/20. For example, he believed that income and wealth throughout history and around the world were distributed in a way that 80% was held by 20% of the people. The application of this same broad theory is helpful when problem solving. What if 20% of your customers were the cause of 80% of your problems? What if 20% of your customers generated 80% of your profits? The way to answer these questions is to collect data, analyze it, and present it graphically on a Pareto Chart.

Allied Security used an application of the Pareto technique in the 1990s. A company with thousands of employees can incur a sizable cost due to on-the-job injuries since the employer must pay for medical care and compensation for lost income when an employee misses work after an accident on the job. At Allied, we tracked the cost of accidents for years on a branch-by-branch basis. We decided to track it by customer location. Sure enough, we found that the bulk of our injuries were taking place at a small percentage of our client properties. This fact makes sense; some sites are inherently more dangerous. We had no way to control the environments where our employees worked, so we could do little to reduce the frequency of accidents at those facilities. When we factored in the cost of accidents at certain client locations, we discovered we had been providing service to those customers for years and losing money. We did two things. First, we let the contracts at the worst locations expire and did not seek renewal. Second, before taking on any new business, we looked at the working conditions to ensure that the place was a reasonably safe place to work. Many times, we are so focused on the trees that we fail to see the forest. If we focused only on getting and maintaining clients, we would lose money at some sites. Our decision to turn down business at some dangerous sites typifies a case where the customer is always right but not every customer is right for you.

Here is one more example. One thing that is worse than having a shortage of customers is to have too many customers who don't pay their bills. In our industry, if we billed a customer $10 an hour for service, eight of those dollars paid for service delivery. If we never collected payment for our services, we lost those $8, a loss that ate up the contribution that four hours of paid-service made toward overhead and profit. We did a Pareto-type review of the customers who generated most of our uncollectable revenue. A pattern became clear. Most of our collection problems came from three types of service users: construction companies, trucking companies, and customer-owned-and-operated businesses. The last group is interesting. Many business owners treat every dollar spent as if it were coming out of their grocery allowance. They are much more inclined to deduct eight hours from the bill arbitrarily because the officer was not wearing his hat properly, or some other minor issue, in order to save money. After our Pareto-type review, we avoided most of the customers who fit into the problem categories and always avoided owner-operator construction companies.

In the next chapter, I discuss a trip to Cleveland and how it brought about the total overhaul of Allied's system for selling its services. One of the tools we used to analyze the problem and plan our solution was a flow chart. This graphical presentation of each step in our sales system showed how each step would be accomplished. The more complicated the steps in performing a service or producing a product, the more valuable the flow chart becomes. It is like a map with a red line marking the route from start to finish.

Pareto charts and flow charts are just two of many tools. Others include check sheets, cause-and-effect diagrams, run charts, histograms, and scatter diagrams.[5] These tools and techniques help users recognize, define, and solve problems. You can explore them to your heart's content. The more you do, the better you'll become at getting things done.

The next step in our problem-solving method is the search for options. When facing a problem, it never helps to utter the words, "What shall we do?" The right words are "What are the options?"

This approach is a more positive and accurate assessment of the situation. There are always options. Understand that if you choose to do nothing, you are still choosing an option.

Get the team together and brainstorm. Clear your mind of all that has been done before and start fresh. Reach back into past experiences. You might find an option based on a hobby or totally different activity. All options voiced are written down, preferably where all team members can see them. There should be minimal discussion at first, only what is necessary to understand the option. Once there are no more options to write down, the fun really begins and more tools come into play.

A continuum can be helpful. Draw a line and place options that appear to have the least potential on the far left and those with higher potential on the right. Slowly narrow the list down. If one option is clearly the best, that option moves forward for deeper analysis. If two or more appear to be equal in potential, they all move forward.

If an option looks like it will solve the problem, it is time for more analysis. The cost and corresponding benefits need detailed examination. An option might be ruled out if it costs more to implement than the benefits that would result. Costs come in many forms. They include obvious things such as money and resources, but the less obvious costs must be factored into the mix, including time required to implement the solution if time is critical, disruption to other important activities, or legal and public relations ramifications. Imagine the nightmare the Takata Corporation faced over its faulty airbags installed in 67 million cars.[6]

There are always options, and one or more will become the solution to a problem. Just as the word "problem" has a negative connotation but is not always negative, the word "solution" has a positive connotation but might be positive only in the sense that it is the best of many bad options.

When the solution has passed all of the required reviews, a detailed plan will help put the solution into place. Without a good plan, the solution might never produce the anticipated and reachable results. The plan is the first stage of the PDCA cycle. From that point on, testing determines whether more work needs to be done on the problem or if the time has come to conclude that the problem is solved.

Problem solving is something we all do every day. Like almost everything else, we can get better at it if we study proven methods and techniques and use them routinely. If we do it for a while, it becomes a habit, and we don't even need to think about it. It becomes automatic. Every individual has wants and needs. The more we get done—the more problems we solve—the more productive we are and the more we will be able to satisfy our wants and needs and those of others.

If you work at becoming a better problem solver, you will also be better able to evaluate the "solutions" politicians are proposing. Too often, they only want to change the people in a system. They have no real plan to change the technology or the process to create a better system. Introduce your children to a methodical approach to dealing with problems. It is a skill that will help them throughout life.

Selected Quotes

"Well, if it can be thought, it can be done, a problem can be overcome."[1]

–Bucchianeri

"Tackle the root cause and not the effect."[1]

–Haresh Sippy

"Leadership is self-made. People who have deliberately decided to become problem solvers lead better."[1]

–Israelmore Ayivor

"It's so much easier to suggest solutions when you don't know much about the problem."[1]

–Malcolm Forbes

"Creating something is about problem solving."[7]

–Philip Seymour Hoffman

"I love leaving the door open to good ideas. I love the collaborative swirl. I get charged by problem solving."[7]

–Ron Howard

"Economists who have studied the relationship between education and economic growth confirm what common sense suggests: The number of college degrees is not nearly as important as how well students develop cognitive skills, such as critical thinking and problem-solving ability."[7]

–Derek Bok

"Problem solving is essential to engineering. Engineers are constantly on the lookout for a better way to do things."[7]

–Dinesh Paliwal

W. Edwards Deming's PDCA Cycle

The PDCA Cycle comes from the scientific model of forming hypotheses and then testing them.[3]

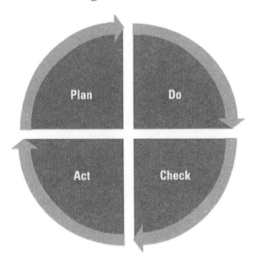

Plan: Establish your objectives and how you plan to achieve them. In the scientific method, the equivalent step is creating your hypothesis and prediction.

Do: Implement the plan. You make it happen. In the scientific method, this step is the test of your hypothesis.

Check: Measure to determine what happened. The scientific method calls this step *the analysis*.

Act: Think about root causes that may explain the difference between actual and planned results. To close the cycle of improvement, act on a new plan to implement and test these root causes. This stage reflects the scientific method's commitment to evaluate and improve.

Chapter 12

"Hiring" Politicians

"Our government, national and state, must be freed from the sinister influence or control of special interests."[1]

–Theodore Roosevelt

I n 1994, I was back in Cleveland visiting Allied Security's branch office. I had started there as a management trainee twenty-one years earlier. My title was now senior vice president. I was responsible for operations and personnel countrywide. The Cleveland office was Allied's first expansion office and had been in operation for about twenty-eight years. I don't remember why I was there, but I remember what happened and the end result.

The branch salesperson for that office had recently left the company. Out of curiosity more than anything else, I asked to see the sales records and wanted to make sure that someone was following up on outstanding sales proposals. What I found, or more accurately, what I didn't find, was a shock. I realized that things had to change and that I had to get involved to make those changes happen.

What I didn't find was one scrap of paper, one file, or one computer entry reflecting sales information after the company had worked that market for twenty-eight years. We had a system that was supposed to prevent this error from happening. The system failed. As a result, after we hired and trained a new salesperson, that person would have to start from scratch identifying potential customers and building a database for each customer. Put another way, our high-priced talent would be collecting data, a task performed at the early stage of selling, instead of making sales calls and presenting proposals. This situation would set back our sales efforts in that market for years.

I called the president of Allied. We had discussed sales problems before, and this situation was the last straw. Together, we decided that I would become an executive vice president and take over sales as well as operations and personnel. The vice president of sales would now report to me.

My first step was to call a meeting at the corporate office and create a team of sales and information technology people to look at our system. It took an hour or two for us to conclude that the best approach would be to start over. We started by creating a diagram that reflected every step related to selling our services and how each step would be accomplished. We used the flow chart mentioned in Chapter 11. We left that first day with the task unfinished because we had differences of opinion.

Everyone was asked to finalize their thoughts and bring them to the next meeting. We worked as a team over several months and drafted a completely new way to run the sales side of our business. We took that draft to all of the salespeople in the company and collected their input. We finalized the program and started phasing it into place. If we discovered flaws, we corrected them. We experienced little to no resistance to the changes because the people who would use the system had been involved in creating it. The system was theirs, and they believed it would make them more productive.

I want to highlight one glaring inconsistency we found in our previous sales system. It is the type of thing one misses when looking only at individual parts of a system. The problem related specifically to sales styles. Companies select a sales style for their salespeople to use in selling their product or service. Job applicants use a "sales style" when they try to convince an employer to hire them. Politicians also use a "sales style" to get you to "hire" them.

I'll start by talking about the two ends of a continuum of selling styles. On the one end is what I call the "slick-'em" approach. The essence of this approach is that the salespeople will resort to almost any measure to make a sale. For them, it's a game. They don't care if the sale is good for the customer or even for the company that employs them. They see sales as a win-lose game, and they want to win. The fact that they get paid to win is also a motivator. Part of their training is to get prospects to talk about what they want and then present a sales pitch that leads prospects to believe they can get everything they want. If the salesperson knows the competition, he might even resort to sneaking in a few reasons why a competitor would be a bad choice. It sounds awful, but doesn't it also sound familiar? This sales style is incompatible with TQM.

On the other end of the continuum is "consultative selling." The objective here is to establish a long-term, win-win relationship. The salesperson's role is to build rapport and trust with the prospect. When the prospect wants to pursue a business relationship, the salesperson is there to provide guidance. Sometimes, the salesperson says "no" to the customer and waits for the right opportunity to start a relationship when the customer is ready for a win-win partnership. This is the sales style that must be used if your objective is a relationship consistent with TQM.

The glaring inconsistency we found was that we wanted to use a consultative sales approach but were putting our salespeople through a popular sales-training program we had purchased that was geared toward the "slick-'em" selling style. It was both unproductive and counterproductive. We had to find and implement a different training program for our salespeople.

In 1783, the American Revolution officially ended with the signing of the Treaty of Paris.[2] Within three years, there was a rebellion of sorts in states from New Hampshire to South Carolina. The source of dissatisfaction was primarily taxation. The rebellion in Massachusetts was the most significant. It started in the western part of the state in April 1786 and lasted until June 1787.[3] Daniel Shays was a farmer and a wounded veteran from the revolution. The rebellion, known as Shays' Rebellion, pitted four thousand men similar to Shays against the merchantmen of the state. The state militia and private forces put down the rebellion and Shays and his compatriots were punished. No federal forces were involved, indicating a major weakness in the Articles of Confederation. The federal government had no ability to tax and, therefore, had to rely on the states to provide funding. This was a source of frustration to George Washington throughout the Revolutionary War. He could never raise enough money to pay soldiers and provide for their welfare. The problem continued after the war.

The root causes of the rebellion are interesting because they are similar to those that have led to unrest and disenfranchisement throughout history. For our purposes, however, the events that resulted from the rebellion are of greater significance.

Put yourself in Daniel Shays' position. He fought in several major battles during the revolution and was wounded. He had been promised pay for his services, but those promises were not met, primarily because the states would not contribute the required funds. He returned to his farm in rural Massachusetts and found that he and many others in the area were losing their land and property to merchants who had granted them credit. Because of their unpaid services during the war and a poor harvest, the farmers were unable to repay their debts. To make matters worse, the state had enacted new taxes that the farmers couldn't pay. That situation, like many, was one where right and wrong were hard to determine, and it set one group against another and with good cause. The merchants were the clear winners, and the farmers were definitely the losers. The problem could have reached resolution with more compassion and less greed, but things did not operate that way then. What had failed was a system for raising the necessary money to pay for a revolution and for federal soldiers to put down a small rebellion. Daniel Shays, after being punished, went to live in rural New York State, where he died in poverty.

As a result of this rebellion and a series of other issues, a meeting was called in Philadelphia to review changes to the Articles of Confederation. Finally, enough of the right people saw that the problems the new government was facing were not going away. Something had to be done. George Washington sensed that he could no longer enjoy his retirement. His decision to come to Philadelphia as a delegate from Virginia might have had more impact on the success of the United States than any other event at that time. Washington was clearly the most respected statesman in the country. He had earned the respect and confidence of his peers through a lifetime of unselfish service. Not surprisingly, he was selected as the president of the Constitutional Convention.[4] He was a man of competence, but much more importantly, he was a man of extraordinary character. He, more than any other person, is the reason that a ragtag army of poorly fed and poorly armed men beat the armed forces of Great Britain. He turned fifty-five delegates from twelve states with different agendas into a team that produced a system of governance that has worked remarkably well for about 230 years. He selflessly set the country on the right path with his eight years of leadership as our first president. Shays' Rebellion was pivotal in our history because it was the catalyst for the events that produced our Constitution.

Before I discuss some options for creating a new system for "hiring" politicians, I need to bring up some ideas I covered earlier. First, I want to bring relativity into the mix again and use a continuum as we have done in other situations. This continuum is a performance rating scale that starts with the number *one* on the far left, has the numbers *two* through *nine* spaced evenly as we move to the right, and ends with the number *ten*. *One* represents the worst imaginable system for hiring politicians in a democracy, and *ten* represents the best system. Just for the sake of relativity, I will place our current system at two on the continuum. I don't think it's a one, but anything higher than three is being generous. We should strive for a ten in a new system, but we need to be realistic and willing to accept that an eight would be tremendous progress. We might even have to settle for a five or a six. In all probability, we will not get to nine or ten because people will debate what is actually better, and like all debates, tradeoffs will come into play. Different people will put different values on each tradeoff. As I discuss an option, therefore, don't examine it as if it were in a vacuum. Consider it in context with other options and the current system. An option might not be great, but it only has to be better than what is currently in place to merit consideration. Also remember that options are not proposals. They are ideas to kick around and see whether they have a place in the eventual solution to a problem.

I will start with a proposal, an idea I strongly believe should be acted upon, and then I will get to the options. If my proposal is adopted, this book will have achieved my primary goal. If all of my options are rejected, I will not mind, especially if they are replaced with better ideas.

Proposal

The president of the United States should establish a committee to review and recommend changes to our federal election system that will do the following:

- Give voters better choices
- Reduce dissension
- Minimize the influence of money
- Have a positive impact on the harmful effects of two-party politics
- Use modern technology in productive and positive ways
- Reduce waste

Rather than address all elections in the United States, I will focus on the "hiring" of the president, vice president, and senators because these offices are arguably the most important at the federal level. My suggestions are transferable to other elections.

The methods for picking the vice president and the senators were changed by amendments to the Constitution, Amendments twelve and seventeen, respectively, indicating that filling these offices was problematic. The problem then and now is not so much the final decision between two contenders for a single job. The problem is all that happens in the system to narrow the choices down to two for president and vice president and two for each senator.

The choice for vice president is an entirely different matter. Citizens do not select the vice president. The candidates for the presidency and their parties make those selections. When voters go to vote, they choose between two teams. The choice of running mates has been a cause for concern throughout our history. The driving force behind the selection has mostly been to produce a balanced ticket that would garner the most votes. This consideration overrode matters such as compatibility, competence, and character. In too many cases, the vice president has played a minor role in governance once the election was over. Such was the case with presidents Franklin Roosevelt, Harry Truman, John F. Kennedy, and Lyndon Johnson. Consider what happened when Abraham Lincoln was assassinated. We went from first to worst.

I have hired hundreds of people and fired hundreds of people. In too many cases, people I fired were the same people I hired. No system works in every situation. The best we can do is create a system that works better than the one it replaced and keep refining it as we go forward. In some ways, less is better. Spending more time and money does not improve outcomes, and in some cases, it adversely affects outcomes.

When I was approaching retirement from Allied, we wanted to hire a national sales and marketing manager. We had identified a strong candidate and were going through the time-consuming process of checking out a few other prospects to make sure we had the best one. Our primary candidate called me and said that he had another offer he would have to take if we didn't make him one. I called the president of the company and got him off the golf course. We put together the offer and presented it that night. He accepted and turned out to be an excellent hire, one we could have lost if he had not chosen to give us one final chance to make our move. When hiring, you are often forced to make compromises. You have to determine how much you are willing to pay in recruiting fees and in your compensation package to find the right people. You have to move quickly but carefully. You also have to acknowledge that some aspects of the system you put in place are not especially appealing, but they are the best of what is available.

Below are some options to consider for improving our election system. Each is followed by comments that explain and/or support my thinking.

Option 1: Limit elections to ninety days or less.

Canada has run a national election campaign in thirty-six days, and its longest campaign ran for about seventy-seven days. Some 61% of Canadians are happy with their governance, and only 40% of Americans are happy with theirs.[5] Other democracies set very specific time limits for campaigns. We should do the same thing, and it should be the shortest possible time span.

It is not easy to count the days of election campaigns in some countries because the actual times when unofficial and official campaigning begin are not definitive. Here are some numbers that should give us reason to wonder about our system. Our last general election campaign ran for over 590 days. In that same time period, Mexico could have run four elections, Canada seven, Great Britain fourteen, Australia fourteen, and France forty-one.[6] It took Georgia sixty-one days to have a runoff election involving two Senate seats when we were already down to only two candidates for each one. Voters endured sixty-one days of TV commercials ad nauseum and daily mailers filled with hate and threats of dire consequences should the opposition win.

At the end of a recent general election cycle, 60% of Americans said they were exhausted by the glut of election coverage.[6] A positive reason given for these long campaigns is that they supposedly give voters more say in who will advance to the final showdown and more knowledge about the candidates. Whether this reason is factual is uncertain. However, a better question is whether the positive elements of these campaigns outweigh the negatives. The long and ugly nature of the system discourages some of the best prospects from running. Voters might have a say in the earlier stages of the system, but many good potential candidates won't enter politics at all. In the end, voters have to pick from the candidates who were the favorites of influential politicians and special-interest groups. As for learning more about the candidates, most of what we learn is how bad things will be if we elect any of them.

We are paying a tremendous price to become involved earlier and still experience an unsatisfactory outcome. Let's explore the costs.

We are discouraging good people from running and exhausting voters to the point that they become disgusted with the game and drop out. The tactics have reached new lows. We repeatedly hear the buzzwords that campaign managers have determined will win the most votes. Polls and focus groups determine the best buzzwords, a tactic taken from "slick-'em" selling, and then bombard voters with their messages. The most ludicrous claim candidates can make is that they can pull the country together and reduce gridlock and discord.

Our election system epitomizes confrontation from start to finish. The result will never pull our country together. The parallels are clear. It is as if Allied Security wanted to build long-term relationships of a win-win nature with customers and used "slick-'em" techniques to start those relationships.

Some selling systems rely on shady tactics. They work best for door-to-door, vacuum-cleaner sales and other one-time sales. Some employers and job candidates go that dark route, but the approach is going out of style. It usually results in adversarial relationships rather than partnerships. It definitely should go out of style in election systems. However big a part of our tradition it is, the time has come for change. The result of the current system is a divided nation, a nation that rarely reaches compromise and where one party does something it thinks is good only to have the other party undo it when it comes to power. The same thing happens repeatedly, making progress impossible.

Because we are talking about costs, let's talk about money. We spend billions of dollars on elections. That money can come from the federal government, political parties, and donations from citizens, corporations, and special-interest groups. In a few cases, it comes from the personal wealth of a candidate. The money follows a convoluted path. For example, a citizen makes a contribution to a special-interest group. That group passes the money on to a political party, and then the party passes it along to a candidate the group favors. Indirectly, every dollar spent is in some way paid for by individual Americans. Many of the dollars paid out will be recovered by way of price increases on the goods and services Americans buy. Other dollars contributed will have a more subtle cost. Special-interest groups will get what they want to the detriment of what the majority of Americans want.

We have a bad system in place, and the less time the system is in high gear, the better off we'll be. If nothing else, a new system would reduce the meaningless rhetoric, cut the potential for the brainwashing cycle to be completed, reduce confrontation, and save money.

This option promotes cutting down the length of campaigns from years to months. We should be able to run a general election in ninety days or fewer.

Option 2: Take money out of the equation using a four-pronged attack.

The first prong is Option 1 above. If we drastically cut the length of the campaigns, costs will decline. Second, we need to use technology in a positive way. The vast majority of funds in elections go to familiarizing voters with the candidates and swaying voters toward a particular candidate, much of them going to methods for manipulating voters. What takes place is vast overkill in both areas. Familiarization is essential, but modern technology can do it in a more practical and cost-effective way. The techniques used to influence voter attitudes have gone beyond absurdity. The only limit on what campaign managers will do in this area is the amount of money they have.

The second and third areas that need addressing are linked. If candidates don't have vast personal wealth, they are forced to beg, and begging is humiliating and compromises the independence of office seekers. This dilemma is destructive because people unwilling to raise funds cannot compete. As the cycle for each general election begins, a few people will "throw their hats in the ring," only, weeks later, to drop their pursuit of public office. In most cases, they could not raise the financial support needed to have any chance of mounting a serious campaign. We are far beyond the point of getting anything of value for all the money that is spent on influencing voters. If we can't control the money, the best thing to do is eliminate it. If the government provided all funding, an equal amount for all candidates, and the only objective was to allow voters the opportunity to learn about each candidate, the cost would be negligible. Government funding, if it were the only source of funds allowed, would also prevent the wealthy from using their own funds to their advantage.

President Theodore Roosevelt was emphatic about prohibiting the flow of money from special-interest groups and corporations into politics. He held that position over one hundred years ago. The situation has worsened. We can take money out of the game if we are willing to change the way the game is played. There is no other way.

Option 3: Stop the debates.

They do far more harm than good, and any attempt to recon-
struct them is sure to fail. Other than a sorry source of entertain-
ment, they serve no useful purpose. Only in politics do two or more
candidates for the same job face off against one another. From the
perspective of a traditional hiring system, this activity is
misleading. It leads the voter to the mistaken belief that debating
skills are a key component in performing as a public servant, when
what we need most from politicians is the ability to pull a group of
people together and get things done through compromise and
teamwork. Perhaps we should vote for the debate loser, especially
if the loser is civil when the other candidate is obnoxious, belittling,
and self-promoting. This idea is comparable to the earlier story
about the Allied branch manager using eye contact in his
evaluation of a secretarial candidate. Using eye contact as a means
of evaluation is okay, but it must be done correctly. Just as good eye
contact is appropriate for an Allied sales candidate and poor eye
contact is appropriate for an Allied secretary, an outlandish
debating performance might demonstrate behavior that is *common*
in the current political arena but not *conducive* to positive outcomes.

Think back also to the story of the Falcons and how they made
a bad decision when hiring a coach who "talked a good game."
They failed to look at his past performance. Today's political debates rarely look at past performance. When they do, the focus is
generally on the other guy's "poor" past performance.

The importance placed on debates is wrong for many reasons.
Past performance is the best indicator of future performance. Debating, in its current form, has nothing to do with past performance. It is all about showmanship and making the other
contenders look bad.

In one of the early TV debates, John F. Kennedy was the perceived
winner because Richard Nixon did not get a good shave before the

show went on the air. In 1980, Ronald Reagan nailed Jimmy Carter with the clever phrase, "There you go again, Jimmy." We should not put so much weight on little things, yet voters frequently do. We are like the assistant security manager at the IRS complex in Boston who rejected a candidate because she couldn't work with someone who didn't make good eye contact. Hiring decisions are better made using the "total-person" concept.

Good hiring decisions come from working your way through a detailed analysis of exactly what the job calls for and measuring the prospects against the job requirements. Voters cannot be expected to do everything that personnel experts are trained to do, but they should understand that they have to do more than base a decision on a five o'clock shadow or the use of a clever phrase to belittle an opponent.

We want to reduce discord and open conflict in government so that we can get more positive things done. Debates put our highest-level politicians on a worldwide stage and encourage them to attack each other. This setup does serious damage to the relationships among the candidates and sends a terrible message around the world. During debates, our leaders and potential leaders set an example of how *not* to behave. Once we have a victor, the celebration speech always contains words like the following: "Now it is time for us to forget our differences and work together." We have not set aside our differences and worked together in a long time, and our system does not permit that cooperation to happen.

Below are some comments by foreigners about the 2020 debate between President Donald Trump and former Vice President Biden.[7]

"This debate would be sheer comedy if it wasn't such a pitiful and tragic advertisement for U.S. dysfunction."

–Kenyan commentator Patrick Gathara

"If last night's presidential debate was supposed to inform and educate, all it did was merely confirm the credibility deficit in U.S. politics, as President Trump and Democrat nominee Joe Biden engaged in what can only be described as a fact-free, name-calling contest."

–Michael Hewson, chief market analyst at CMC Markets in the United Kingdom

"An election debate in the States last night, where the interruptions and quarrels were allowed to fill up way too much . . . the harsh words polarize and split."

–Danish Prime Minister Mette Frederiksen

"The impression is that of a country in stalemate, paralyzed by politics and tones that are foreign to its tradition."

–Walter Veltroni, former mayor of Rome, Italy

"I think it was something extraordinarily upsetting because people want to be able to look to America to lead and to guide and to role model."

–Leslie Vinjamuri, director of U.S. and American programs at a London think tank

"Spiteful, chaotic, abusive, often out-of-control brawling encounter with both candidates revealing their contempt for each other."

–Paul Kelly, Australian political journalist

These quotes come from countries that are allies. I didn't include a quote from an editor of a newspaper in China because you would expect it to be critical, and you would be right.

Political debates are a tradition we no longer need. They have deteriorated to such an extent that it makes no sense to try to fix them. The best solution is to stop having them.

Option 4: End the sabotage of one candidate by another.

The debates are only one of the forums in which candidates have become accustomed to disrespecting the opposition. The tactics of undermining the opponent are visible in almost every TV commercial, speech, and printed material used in a campaign. All of the rules of civility are ignored. "All is fair in love and war" needs expanding: "All is fair in love, war, and politics, unless you make it impossible in politics." The behavior of candidates in all aspects of the campaign should be exemplary in every way and deplorable in no way. We have it backwards, and the results are as follows:

- The leaders we need will not roll in the mud, behavior that the game now requires.
- Public servants set out on long campaign trails instead of doing their jobs.
- Competitors end up hating each other, yet we expect them to work together.
- Voters learn what is bad about candidates more than what is good.
- Sabotage divides the population further.
- Sabotage spreads the mistaken belief that incivility is admirable conduct.

- Sabotage damages the image of our leaders in the eyes of leaders around the world.
- Respect for America and Americans is eroding around the world.

We are supposed to be the champions of democracy. We want to send a message to the world that democracy is the best form of governance. Our president is frequently called the leader of the free world, sometimes the most powerful person in the world. Our humiliating conduct, especially the debates during elections, does not project the impression we want to make on the world.

Option 5: **Provide citizens with information on how to derive the most from their right to vote.**

The subject matter would include material from this book and similar sources that explain how to evaluate people. It would teach how not to become caught up in the myths and common misconceptions that many people use when evaluating other people for employment, contract work, or public office. The lessons have many applications, so time spent getting educated is time well spent. Critical points would include the following: past performance is the best indicator of future performance, look at the total person, and make sure you have a clear idea about the type of person who can best perform the task.

With current technology, the materials could be cheaply and readily available on the internet or in print form on request. The main message should be that to make a wise and informed decision, you have to dig into reliable historical records to find the facts. The facts will not come from TV news or documentaries. Most of that material is biased, and its producers want to entertain you. News and documentaries might contain more hype than substance. Forget social media as a source of facts.

Option 6: Put technology to *good* use.

Don't make an already bad situation worse. TV and social media have been enthusiastically incorporated into our election system and overwhelmed voters with negative messages. This technology could have cut the time of campaigns from fifteen or sixteen months to two or three months. Election campaigns have only one legitimate objective: to familiarize voters with politicians running for office. Instead, campaigns now provide disinformation and scare voters.

Voter familiarization could be accomplished by preparing two videos of each candidate. One would be three minutes long and permit the candidate to talk about himself and no one else. The second video would be thirty minutes long. Candidates would cover three topics: ideals, capabilities, and character. Candidates can choose how to reveal this information as long as they make no reference to other candidates. All videos would be uploaded to the internet at the same time, about sixty days before election day. Voters could look at the three-minute videos, pick the candidates they like most, and then screen their thirty-minute videos. Candidates would be finished campaigning.

There would be no debates, no appearances on TV, and no in-person appearances. There would be no mailers or newspaper or magazine interviews. The government would bear the cost of the videos. The cost of elections would decrease from billions to thousands. No more begging for bucks. Special-interest groups would have to throw more money at their lobbyists instead of the media. TV producers would have to find other programming to keep us entertained.

I haven't touched the surface of what we could do with today's technology in terms of voting and counting votes. In the last election, early voting and mail-in voting became subjects of intrigue. I have been voting by mail for years to elect corporation board members. I can securely make all types of financial transactions with my bank from my home. I can call my stock brokerage firm and say three words to confirm my identity through voice-recognition technology. We apply technology in piecemeal fashion. Politicians used to go on the campaign trail to get in front of voters. Now they go on TV. We buy better voting machines and put them in polling places that used to be the only place we could collect and count votes. We can easily create a secure method to vote from home on a telephone or computer. People who in the past had difficulty getting to the polls or didn't want to wait in line would perhaps vote for the first time. We could avoid crowds. A built-in system could count votes. Such a system would also open the door for us to switch to ranked-choice vote counting, if we wished to make that change as well.

Too often, technology is used against us rather than for us. Political campaigning is one example. Robocalls are another. We now have technology to stop our phones from ringing when we get a robocall. Technology to stop technology. I am not sure we can stop robocalls entirely, but we should deal with the rest of the nonsense that technology creates during elections.

We need to use new technology to cut the time and cost of elections and give us the same or a far better outcome. We have the technology we need. We have to use it to achieve the right goals. The wrong goals are scaring, angering, misleading, discouraging, brainwashing, and belittling people.

Option 7: Create a powerful Federal Election Commission.

The current commission has too narrow a purpose. The president selects members, and the Senate confirms them. These people are the same ones whom the commission should be overseeing. This group should set the standards for the entire election system at the federal level. It could establish the dates for campaigns and the way the system operates during the campaign. It would enforce the rules. It would have to review the effectiveness of the system and coordinate appropriate changes. One of its most difficult tasks would be to figure out the best way to narrow down the field of candidates to a manageable number for each position. The group could then use the resources of the FBI to investigate the backgrounds of all candidates, before they come before voters, to ensure they meet all of the requirements for the office they seek. Doing so would avoid situations where the citizenship of a candidate becomes a debatable issue, for instance. If a standard were set that candidates must present their tax returns, the commission would enforce that requirement. We do not have to reinvent the wheel. Other countries use election commissions. We can learn from their experience. Using the "best practices" of others demonstrates our respect for others and the value we see in them.

Here's a brief story. Allied was meeting with the security people from a large corporation. The subject of TQM came up. One of the security managers mentioned a great video his group was trying to obtain to train staff. I asked him if he would like to borrow ours. He lifted his eyebrows and said, "That's a joke, right?" He could not believe a lowly uniform guard service contractor would have a library of videos on TQM. We provided the video. Being the most powerful person in the room doesn't mean that you cannot receive valuable help from the little guys.

Our election system needs management. It can only come from a group dedicated to that task and no other. At present, the system is without a leader.

My seven options are just a starting place for more brainstorming and exhaustive analysis. Below, I have summarized the results—the symptoms of the problem—of our current election system. As you examine the list, remember that these are the cracks on the surface. We must trace them back to their causes. Those root causes will be our targets for correction.

Election System Results

1. Gridlock, "doing-and-undoing," and waste
2. People of wrong character hired; people of right character discouraged
3. Billions of dollars spent to empower special-interest groups and compromise officeholders
4. Promises made to deceive and manipulate voters
5. Debates that do far more harm than good
6. Polls to see what voters want and poll results used in "slick-'em" sales tactics
7. Culture of disrespect and distrust in and out of government
8. Many hate-filled losers
9. A system that continues to worsen instead of improving
10. People rewarded through the "spoils" system
11. Unhappy, frustrated, and angry citizens
12. Loss of respect for America around the world

———

I'll close this chapter by reminding readers of several important points.

First, I made only one proposal. The seven options are areas to think about. Other options are welcome.

Second, don't forget relativity. The issue is not whether any of these options are any good or make any sense. The issue is whether our current system is doing anything good for us and whether the changes make more sense.

Third, there will be tradeoffs no matter what we do. One big one will be how we narrow down the list of candidates. Nothing has worked well to date. We have to try something different. Again, the question is not how bad those tradeoffs are but whether they are better than the tradeoffs that come with the system in place.

Fourth, some things are easy to do, while others will be much harder. Two things are relatively easy: cut the length of campaigns and stop the debates.

Finally, education is critical to this effort. We live in a complicated and interconnected world. Simple solutions to difficult problems are few, if they exist at all. If anyone thinks up a simple answer and happens to be right, that person is a genius, and there are far too few geniuses, especially in politics. People who think the answer is obvious are usually wrong because they are uninformed. The more educated citizens are, the more clearly they will see reality and the more willing they will be to compromise.

Work at becoming an informed voter and better at hiring people. Just as you teach your children to drive, teach them how to participate in a democracy. And if you do a good job of teaching them how to get hired, you might avoid having one of your adult children living rent-free in your basement.

Selected Quotes[8]

"There is absolutely no circumstance whatever under which I would accept that spot. Even if they tied and gagged me, I would find a way to signal by wiggling my ears."

–Ronald Reagan on the Vice Presidency

"All that Hubert needs over there is a gal to answer the phone and a pencil with an eraser on it."

–Lyndon Johnson on his Vice President

"I just received the following wire from my generous Daddy: 'Dear Jack, Don't buy a single vote more than is necessary. I'll be damned if I'm going to pay for a landslide.'"

–John Kennedy

"If I were two-faced, would I be wearing this one?"

–Abraham Lincoln

"If one morning I walked on top of the water across the Potomac River, the headline that afternoon would read: 'President Can't Swim.'"

–Lyndon Jonson on the News Media

"Politics is supposed to be the second-oldest profession. I have come to realize that it bears a very close resemblance to the first."

–Ronald Reagan

Chapter 13

Bigger Changes

"If you want to change the world,
pick up your pen and write."[1]

–Martin Luther

"Change almost never fails because it's too early.
It almost always fails because it is too late."[2]

–Seth Godin

"Never doubt that a small group of thoughtful, committed
citizens can change the world. Indeed, it is the only thing
that ever has."[3]

–Margaret Mead

"Education is the most powerful weapon
you can use to change the world."[3]

–Nelson Mandela

> "Any change, even for the better, is always accompanied by drawbacks and discomfort."[3]
>
> **–Arnold Bennett**

As I have done for each of the chapters in this book, I searched for an appropriate quote to start the chapter. With so many great quotes about change, I could not pick just one.

This book is all about the need to make changes and how to make changes happen. I have already discussed the need to make some significant changes to our governance system, especially the way we conduct elections. If you thought the changes covered thus far were big, what follows might cause you to reconsider.

If we can solve the problems with our election system and get people in office who work together to get the right things done, they can explore many more areas of change. My ideas are wild, crazy, radical, and a bunch of other adjectives you might choose. I know others support some of my ideas. I have to take all of the blame for one or two. They are options. Options can be almost anything, as long as they make a positive contribution toward problem solving. Before reviewing these changes, take a look at a "Hierarchy of Change."

Bringing about change can be impossible or quite easy. On the "impossible" level of the hierarchy would be changing an indisputable fact.

The diameter of a circle will go around the circumference of that circle π times, an immutable fact. The symbol π is the Greek letter *pi*. The value of *pi* is approximately 3.14. Any effort to change *pi* is wasted effort. But that has not stopped some politicians from trying. In 1897, Indiana tried.[4] As we well know, for politicians, there is some confusion about what is a fact and what is not. Some historical facts are generally acknowledged as true (e.g., George Washington was the first president of the United States).

At the "easy-to-change" level are ideas based on ignorance. With a picture of the earth taken from outer space, we should easily be able to convince a child that the earth is round and not flat.

Most ideas fit between the two extremes. As an example, where would the disputed idea that Donald Trump did not win the 2020 presidential election fall? Would it be easy or hard to change that idea in the minds of voters? The level of difficulty depends on the political leaning of the individual voter and how receptive that voter is to the slogan "Stop the Steal."

The Hierarchy of Change diagram at the end of this chapter graphically presents the levels of difficulty we face when we try to make changes. The placement on the diagram indicates what we are up against to make change happen. We could bury ourselves in the small details. What matters is that some things will be easier to change than others. We must take the level of difficulty into consideration when we pick objectives. The position on the diagram will also influence how we attempt to make changes.

Each change I mention below will be extraordinarily difficult, but some will be less so than others. The degree of difficulty doesn't alter the justification for tackling these problems. They are problems that adversely affect our nation. They merit consideration.

States' Rights

The issue of states' rights versus the rights of the federal government has been a source of conflict since any semblance of unity came to the colonies in America. The Articles of Confederation failed largely because the issue of states' rights prevented the creation of a workable system of governance. The states were unwilling to give the federal government a way to collect money, an idea that failed when the federal government needed to fund an army to fight the British. The same issue was the primary sticking point during the Constitutional Convention and is the explanation for much of what emerged.

Separating the two issues that put the North and the South at war in 1861 is difficult: slavery and states' rights. Our history with slavery and the way we have dealt with the aftermath remain a source of major difficulty. Progress in the right direction has been slow and painful. Unfortunately, the same is not true about states' rights. Circumstances connected to states' rights have worsened.

The federal government has steadily, and with the consent of the majority of Americans, taken on an increasingly large role in making decisions that affect all citizens. The trend picked up speed in the early 1900s and has been gaining momentum ever since: national income tax, World War I, the New Deal, World War II, expanded worldwide trade, involvement in programs tied to security, energy, education, health care, and conservation. These initiatives, and many others, have all extended the power and control of the federal government. Many Americans are unhappy with the situation. They don't want to relinquish control of so many aspects of their lives, and they don't like the resulting tax burden.

The many are not the majority, however. Most Americans want the things the federal government provides. Unless we want to undo programs and the bureaucracy that comes with them, we are stuck with the situation—and with systems that are out of date and tend not to work.

In our beginning, states had more power than the federal government, and we made it work. We progressed to the point where the powers were about equal, and we were still able to make it work. Now we have come to the point where the federal government needs to have more power than any single state or any collection of states, and it does not, so things that need to be done are not getting done. Our federal government has evolved into an institution that our Constitution was not designed to accommodate.

Something has to change.

When Americans picked a president and a vice president in 2020, they filled the only two positions in the country where the officeholders report to (are and should be accountable to) all Americans. No other elected official has a responsibility to all citizens. Management has a principle that when you want to hold an individual or a group accountable for an activity, that person or group must have the authority necessary to set in motion the steps that will determine the success or failure of that activity. We have two chambers of Congress that include 535 individuals, and not a single one has the authority or can be rightfully held accountable for doing anything to help this country as a whole. We see the proof of that flaw every day.

Voters need to put in power more people who have a higher level of authority and the responsibility to represent the interests of all Americans. In his book *A More Perfect Constitution*, Larry Sabato proposed a new office of "national senators" made up of former presidents and vice presidents. His aim is similar to mine. An option worth consideration is senior senator positions within the Senate. There should be no fewer than ten and no more than twenty. All voters would elect senior senators. They would be responsible to all voters for what happens across the nation. In addition to making a larger group of people responsible for what happens at the federal level, the position would have two other clear advantages. It would create a logical career path to the presidency. Many presidents came from the Senate to the White House. Another step into the role of a senior senator would give them more experience working for all Americans. The second thing it would do is give voters better visibility of potential candidates for vice president and president.

Donald Trump's election in 2016 tested the theory that someone outside politics might make a good president. He was the first president who had no experience in public service or as a senior military officer, which requires interaction with politicians. I believe voters elected him because of their anger, frustration, and desperation. We should think carefully before we test that theory again. The world and politics have become so complex that only those with experience should apply for top political jobs. We don't have the luxury of allowing on-the-job training. We cannot afford novice errors. We need to base our "hiring" on past experience relevant to the job.

Anger, frustration, and desperation are understandable emotional reactions, but they rarely accomplish anything good. We need more people elected to high office who are in the national spotlight and have proved to all Americans that they are worthy of a promotion.

Having senior senators would overcome the imbalance in our governance system. The federal government has vastly increased its responsibilities since 1789. We need to find ways to get more politicians working for the good of the entire country. It can happen when more politicians are accountable to all of the nation's voters.

Federal Election Commission

With states' rights, the issue is power distribution between the states and the federal government. With our election system, the problem is that no person or group takes responsibility for the system. The system at the federal level falls under the president, but the only time there is any discussion about the workings of the system is when a candidate doesn't like the outcome. Even then, most of the debate is about the electoral college or some other small facet of the system. There is talk about voter fraud, inaccurate counting, mail-in votes, campaign financing, and so forth. If changes come from these efforts, however, they are stop-gap measures with too many holes in the dike. We can't plug the holes fast enough, and nobody admits that the dike needs to be replaced. The entire system is inefficient, ineffective, demoralizing, and embarrassing. Someone needs to take charge. My approach is different.

The federal government has three parts or branches: Congress (the legislative branch), the President (the executive branch), and the Supreme Court (the judicial branch). The Federal Election Commission (FEC) has been around since 1974. It is not getting the job done. We need a group to take responsibility for the election system and do whatever it takes to create a system that works now and improves as time passes. The president selects FEC members whom the Senate must confirm. That system hasn't worked. Of the three branches, two consist of elected officials and one does not. This situation is interesting from a problem-solving viewpoint. It makes sense that the election system must be overseen by one of the three branches of government. We have only three options to consider, and frankly, it is a choice of which of the three is the best of three undesirable alternatives.

We should give the Supreme Court the task of selecting FEC members.

I warned you that these ideas would be wild, but we must try something different. I hope someone has a better idea, but one way or another, we have to get the system under control and manage it, instead of letting it move aimlessly along.

National Service

More than seventy-five countries have some type of requirement for citizens to serve their country. The spectrum runs from as little as one month of service to as many as ten years. Many require service in the range between four months and twenty-four months. Most require service of all able-bodied young adults of both genders, but the length of service might vary between men and women.[5]

France started requiring only one month of service in 2019,[5] time devoted to learning certain skills. The country encourages all participants to volunteer for more service to the state after they complete the one month of mandatory service.

Former President Trump commissioned a multi-year study of our Selective Service System. All men are required to register with the Selective Service within thirty days of their eighteenth birthday. The commission affirmed this requirement in 2020 and recommended that the requirement be expanded to include women, but that expansion has not happened yet.[6]

Throughout history, America has had times when men were required to serve in the armed forces, a system known as the draft. The last draft ended in 1973.[7] The draft had many inequities. We should never go back to any similar system. However, we should take a hard look at Universal National Service (UNS).

Young adults would be required to serve the country, but not only in the armed forces. They could serve in a wide variety of capacities, ranging from unskilled to very skilled, depending on their interests, aptitude, and time they are willing to serve. The more time they are willing to serve, the more training they would be eligible to receive. I could see young adults as assistant teachers, nursing assistants, and maintenance and repair workers.

Contractors provide security for many government properties. TSA employees at airports once were contracted. Many prisons use contractors to staff their facilities. Personnel with minimal training can easily handle these entry-level positions. In these occupations, turnover of people is desirable so we are realizing a benefit from the use of those performing their national service. For example, one of the biggest problems in prison security is keeping guards from getting too familiar with prisoners. The same is true at other facilities where guards become too friendly with employees they are supposed to check during entry and departure.

UNS would have many benefits. We could realize tremendous cost savings in manpower and recruiting. We could move young people out of difficult homes and away from detrimental peer pressure. We would educate and train young people to be responsible and productive. Years ago, when teenagers got into trouble or dropped out of school, they went into the military. Judges sometimes even forced errant young men to join the military. The military no longer wants these troublemakers. UNS could be an answer to that situation, too.

The overarching objective is to have young people leave UNS with a greater appreciation for what they have and the realization that they should continue to give back to the country that has given them so much. All citizens need to understand that our society is not about how much they can take out of the system. Our society requires giving, compromise, cooperation, mutual respect, understanding, and compassion.

Term Limits

I agree with others who recommend term limits, but I want to see them implemented in connection with a performance rating system. Of the senators in office in 2021, forty-eight of the one hundred were in the House of Representative before becoming senators. In essence, they were promoted from the lower chamber to the upper chamber of Congress. Having senior senators would give senators another rung on the ladder to aspire to ascend. An adaptation of the up-or-out system of the military would be interesting to explore.

What follows is an example of what I am thinking. I used an arbitrary term limit of twelve years for all members of Congress. As any members of Congress reach the twelfth year of service in the same status, they have to seek reelection at a least one rung higher on the ladder. At the end of twelve years, a representative would have to seek reelection as a senator. After twelve years, a senator would have to seek reelection as a senior senator. And after twelve years, a senior senator would have to leave Congress but could strive for a position at the cabinet level or higher.

We should keep the people who have the drive and capability to move up and eliminate those who don't have the capacity or the drive in order to make room for those who do. The more people we have in Congress who realize they have to appeal to all voters if they want to stay in the system and have a shot at the upper echelons of government, the better off we will be.

Cultural Change

We need a major attitude adjustment. First, we need to change our attitude about change itself. We need to pursue change because progress does not come without it. A place to start and clearly demonstrate that we are much more open to change now would be to alter the process for making changes to the Constitution. The modifications could be as small as dropping the requirement for a two-thirds vote to 55% to propose an amendment and cutting the requirement for ratification from 75% to 60%. That small change would facilitate getting things done and would send the important message that changes are welcome.

We need a new attitude with regard to conflict. The writers of the Constitution built in a system of checks and balances with the three branches of government. They did not build into our governance a two-party system that gives us conflict and another set of checks and balances. The parties now check and balance each other to a far greater extent than the branches check and balance each other.

The parties, the ones that George Washington warned us about, are the primary cause of gridlock. The secondary cause is the people who get elected and follow the party line. A change to this culture is essential if we are to improve how the federal government conducts business. Engineering that change will take some masterful problem solvers.

The Spoils System

The spoils system is another tradition that we can do without. Virtually every newly elected politician rewards people who have been helpful and loyal. One of the common rewards is a cushiony government job with a big government salary and benefits package.

The more we can cut down on the number of people required to run a campaign, the more we can reduce the rewards that flow out. As an added benefit, removing the spoils system could increase the competence and character of people paid by our tax dollars to serve our interests.

Prioritizing

The federal government does a poor job of strategizing. It takes up more projects when others are incomplete and, in too many cases, not working as intended. If they approached all of these undertakings with a sense of control and priority, the system would be okay; however, they have not shown the ability to exercise that kind of control. We need to take a step back and look at what is not working and make one of three choices: put forth the effort to get it working, put it on hold with a realistic hope that the project can be successfully completed in a reasonable timeframe, or shut it down.

Franklin Roosevelt had to prioritize to bring about victory in

World War II. He made some painful but essential decisions. He had to get the right things done in the right sequence. Our federal government needs to do the same thing now and will probably always have to prioritize. We don't have unlimited resources.

When managing the affairs of a family or business, some type of budget usually forces the priority setting. A good friend made this wonderful remark about family budgeting: "I hate budgets; they're so confining." Our federal government does not appear to understand budgeting, and sooner or later we will have to face the consequences. We need to prioritize and shut down projects that don't work.

Five factors tie into the hierarchy of change: idealism, morals, religion, individual rights, and money. All five inhibit the implementation of change, but changes are necessary and doable. In the short term, we might be doing far more harm than good by not prioritizing and, instead, doing what seems idealistically right. FDR's decision to sacrifice the war effort in the Pacific so that we could win the war in Europe is a perfect example. In some cases, idealistic projects that many people considered morally right turned out to be disasters. Prohibition, for example, was an ill-conceived and poorly executed program. It attempted to force all Americans to do something unacceptable to too many people. In the grand scheme of things going on in 1919, the government should never have given prohibition such a high priority to move through the amendment process.

We need to take a deep look at our laws, and the results of those laws, related to drug use, gambling, and prostitution. We need to examine the cost/benefit relationship, the short-and long-term probability of success, and whether the time is right to try to solve those types of problems when we have many other more serious problems. If we shifted assets away from enforcing such laws and used those assets to deal with other needs of our society, think of the good things we could accomplish! Consider the tax revenue we could generate. These three issues are moving more under the control of states, but the more the federal government can do to accelerate that move, the better.

Another aspect of priority setting needs addressing. We live in a democracy where the majority makes the decisions. We need to be more accepting of the changes that the majority makes. It is fine to disagree, and disagreement is a right. But refusing to comply or resorting to violence to express disagreement is not a right. Revising or reversing decisions in lawful and civil manners is a right, but weighing the costs and the benefits of doing so is wise. There might be many other things that you would also like to change, and they might be much easier to change. Make those issues your priority. Democracy cannot and will not work if each citizen picks the rules to follow and the rules to violate.

Here is a final area to consider related to prioritizing. Whenever a lower level of government can take on the responsibility of dealing with a problem, it should. The federal government has a constantly full plate. If something could be done better or just as well at the state level, the states should take on the task. Even if the task might not be done as well at the state level, delegation might still be justifiable. Two areas to consider are education and gun control.

I have listed seven areas of change. These are general areas to explore. They are not as specific as the options in Chapter 12. There is some overlap. Both lists are starting points.

We have avoided change in too many areas of governance for far too long. The work ahead of us is mind-boggling. We must recognize the problems, however, and solve them by doing things differently. Changing our election system is a good place to start. You can personally help bring about the first step in changing our election system by honoring a simple request. I will conclude the book with that request.

Selected Quotes[3]

"What's dangerous is not to evolve."

–Jeff Bezos

"When you blame others, you give up
your power to change."

–Robert Anthony

"Only the wisest and stupidest of men never change."

–Confucius

"A fanatic is one who can't change his mind
and won't change the subject."

–Winston Churchill

"Nothing endures but change."

–Heraclitus

"Intelligence is the ability to adapt to change."

–Stephen Hawking

"Progress is a nice word. But change is its motivator. And change has enemies."

–Robert F. Kennedy

"The people who are crazy enough to think they can change the world are the ones who do."

–John McAfee

"Ignorance is always afraid of change."

–Jawaharlal Nehru

"Change happens by listening and then starting a dialogue with the people who are doing something you don't believe is right."

–Jane Goodall

"Change before you have to."

–Jack Welch

"Progress is impossible without change, and those who cannot change their mind cannot change anything."

–George Bernard Shaw

Hierarchy of Change Diagram

Graphically presented below are six separate degrees of difficulty for making changes. It is a guide and nothing more. Explanations and examples follow.

1. Very Changeable
- Ignorance
- Routines

2. Changeable
- Systems, Processes
- Illogical Conclusions
- Twisted "Facts"

3. Moderately Changeable
- Habits
- Acceptable Civic Interaction
- Preferences
- Legislated Laws
- Philosophical Concepts
- Customs and Traditions
- Culture
- Institutions

4. Slightly Changeable
- Deeply Held Beliefs
- Deeply Held Opinions
- Deeply Held Attitudes

5. Almost Unchangeable
- Basic Individual Behavior

6. Unchangeable
- Facts
- Human Nature
- Laws of Nature

Each block represents an area of difficulty to bring about changes. Level 1 is the easiest, and Level 6 is virtually impossible. In the areas listed in Levels 1–3, success is more probable. Level 4 changes will be few and difficult to realize. Changes in the areas in Levels 5 and 6 would be miraculous.

Levels

1. Education can change ignorance. With greater effort, it can offset stupidity. The types of training the armed forces give recruits is great at changing routines.

2. Systems and processes should be designed to be changed as technology and concepts change. With a culture that naturally pursues change, improving is easier. Faulty logic and twisted facts, especially common myths and brainwashed facts, are harder to change, but patience and compassion can accomplish the goal.

3. Here are examples of hard changes to make:
   a. Habits: Exercise regularly, stop biting nails
   b. Acceptable civic Interaction: Treat others with respect and understanding
   c. Preferences: Become a vegetarian
   d. Legislated laws: Legalize drugs
   e. Philosophical concepts: Tell children they can do anything they work for
   f. Customs and traditions: Celebrate Independence Day on July 4
   g. Culture: Adopt teamwork as the best way to get things done
   h. Institutions: Change the way Congress does business

4. Deeply held beliefs about individual rights, religion, and self-appraisal are hard to change.

5. Basic individual behavior, such as values, morality, and introversion versus extroversion, are extremely hard to change.

6. Facts, true facts, are not changeable. Human nature is not worth any effort to change. Humans are greedy. Individuals differ in what satisfies their greed, but self-actualization, at the top of Maslow's Hierarchy of Needs, is another way of saying humans want to be what they believe they are. Communism has a problem trying to get people to be something—for example generous and sharing—that is against their nature. Communist leaders have tried re-education and tried force. So far, human nature is the winner. The laws of nature are as impossible to change as are facts. My favorite law of nature is this: The law of relativity states that you cannot define something without having something to compare it to.[8]

Conclusion

"For an objective approach to a problem, you need to have an overview rather than involvement." [1]

–Haresh Sippy

I've tried to be objective while examining America's problems, especially our election system. Our problems are so broad, however, that as an American, I cannot remain uninvolved. These problems are unsettling. I would much prefer to be doing something else instead of writing this book, but my nature will not permit me to sit back and watch as one ridiculous political event unfolds after another.

Just today, March 5, 2021, it was announced that National Guard troops would remain on duty in Washington D. C. to protect the Capitol from domestic terrorists for the next few months. [2] A few years ago in South America, I saw armed soldiers on patrol in several city centers. I saw the same thing when I visited Russia and Egypt. I never thought it would be commonplace in Washington.

We are treating the occupation of National Guard troops as the new normal while we go about our business as if everything were fine. Our politicians have become more entrenched than ever in party politics and hateful dialogue. President Biden is busy with the undoing of the Trump presidency. The pitiful cycle continues to take us from one extreme to the other. There is no meaningful discussion of the severity of our problems, much less the root causes. We continue to do what we have been doing and expect a good outcome. We are dreaming. We have no reason to believe we are headed toward sweet dreams and many reasons to believe we are on a path to nightmares.

In an effort to help solve America's problems, I can offer only my experiences in hiring people and some knowledge and practice in using TQM to solve problems. I have neither the capability nor the desire to try to deal with our governmental difficulties. The task of getting our governance back on track is comparable to the task the Constitutional Convention faced. It is not quite as large in scope, but it is more difficult because we haven't even reached the point where we recognize we have a problem that needs confronting. In addition, as divided as those fifty-five delegates were in 1787, our country is more divided now than it was at the start of the Constitutional Convention and anytime since the Civil War.

Our system of governance is failing us. The election of 2020 and all that has happened since are symptoms of a problem. One aspect of that overall system failure is a terribly flawed election system. The election system is my primary target for change.

I never intended to propose a solution to any specific problem. Solutions must come from a wide range of experts working together as a team. My intent has been to present Step One and Step Two of a problem-solving method and apply it to elections.

Chapter 1 was about coming to the realization that a problem exists. Nothing gets done without that first step, and that step hasn't been taken.

In the second chapter, I discussed Step Two. The right solution will emerge only after accurately defining the problem. If we can get to Step Two and put together a group to work on the problem, that group's first major chore will be the preparation of a problem definition, the mission statement for the group.

Near the end of Chapter 6, I made a stab at defining the election problem. It was for illustrative purposes more than anything. I tried to explain how things have been done up until now and how they might be done in the future. The entire book has only one *Proposal*. It is spelled out in Chapter 12. Only one individual can take action to resolve our election difficulties. That individual is the *President*. We citizens of America must direct his attention to this issue and request his help.

The options I presented are intended to trigger open-minded thinking and demonstrate that every problem has options. They might not be as good as we'd like, but if they are the best available and better than what is in place, they point toward a solution for now. We can then analyze the results and strive for constant improvement.

If we can get a good start on a problem and show some progress, the people who resisted changes originally will be more likely to accept future proposals for change.

I have included jokes and funny stories, but not because the situation isn't serious or because I have taken it lightly. The opposite is true. The situation is so serious that we will need to do everything we can to lighten the burden. I have added humor as one might add sugar to help distasteful medicine go down.

Our governance system, especially our election system, is in failing health. When the Capitol was assaulted on January 6, 2021, our governance system was theoretically rushed to the emergency room in critical condition. After the assault was quelled, the system was moved into the Intensive Care Unit. It emerged from the ICU on January 20 with a somewhat peaceful but shameful transition of power.

The nation's welfare still requires much needed care, care that most citizens don't even realize is necessary. If we want to recover and become robust, we have to take some powerful and unpleasant medicine. That medicine is **CHANGE.** We have to stop doing the same things over and over. We must realize that the conditions that put us in the ICU have not changed. We will be back in the ICU soon, unless we devise an appropriate treatment plan. As awful as that treatment might be, it might put us on a path to recovery and even better health.

Our governance system is due for many changes because we have perceived the absence of change as a good thing, when it is not. It is frequently necessary when problem solving to prioritize. We need to start with the things that are important but easier. Each success we achieve makes the next one more palatable and improves morale.

I focused on our election system because it is largely based on traditions and, therefore, somewhat easier to change. It will be a beast to change, but relative to some other changes that might help us, it is on the easy end of the continuum.

Here are eight of the goals we should strive for in our elections:

1. Make the election system attractive to individuals of any income level whose past performance has demonstrated competence and character.

2. Give voters choices of candidates who have differing ideals but who are reflective of the majority of Americans, not always the extremes.

3. Seek political candidates with a history of doing what is right and in the best interests of most Americans, not only what is good for a small part of the population.

4. Minimize the power of the parties by placing emphasis on independent thinking and positions more toward the middle. Reduce the doing and undoing after a change in power.

5. Reduce the influence of money and special-interest groups.

6. Cut the harmful rhetoric and decrease dissension.

7. Make positive use of technology and get rid of the negative uses.

8. Decrease the amount of time and the amount of taxpayer money spent by incumbents seeking reelection.

If we can get to Step One and agree there is a problem, we can get good people to look at the situation. The following three elements will be valuable in any solution:

1. **Research:** Every democracy around the world deals with the same problems. Some have found ideas that work. When we look at our history and that of other countries that had systems that did not work, we can learn a great deal. Many countries followed our example when setting up their democracies and then made changes to suit their circumstances. We can learn from them just as they learned from us. This learning could also produce new relationships from which all can benefit, in the short term and the long term.

2. **Education:** Too many Americans think the system is what it is and nothing can be done. It is the only system they have known. They don't think they have a choice. We have to show them other, potentially much better, ways to select and elect candidates. Americans know the system leaves them dissatisfied,

but they don't know why or what can be done. We have to let them know that change is desirable and doable and that their dissatisfaction matters. Once we move toward a new system, education will be essential so that voters understand and accept any necessary tradeoffs and understand their role in making the system produce the results they expect.

3. **Federal Election Commission:** Without someone in charge, no meaningful change will have a lasting effect. Our election system is devoid of leadership. The system changes freely as those in power make changes more suitable for politicians than for citizens. It is worse than a system out of control. It is a system manipulated by the people the system should control. The foxes are fighting one another for control of the hen house (Congress and the White House) while the farmers (citizens) choose which party of foxes will spread havoc in their neighborhood.

One final point I wish to emphasize is the value of Universal National Service. Almost fifty years have passed since the draft ended. I was seventeen in 1961, and the draft was in effect. It influenced my thinking about college. I was likely to end up in the service, one way or another, so I chose to pursue an appointment to West Point. I preferred to be an officer and liked going to a college that paid me. I have never regretted that decision.

Of more significance to the issue of National Service, I have met hundreds of people who were drafted, and few regret their time of service unless they experienced the worst of combat. The National Service I envision would not simply be to staff the armed forces. It would include ways to serve the nation and educate individuals in a wide variety of endeavors. It would be a win-win situation. The individual would get an opportunity to leave the protective nest of home, learn about life, and gain work experience. The nation would get valuable work done in important areas and increase the chances that young adults will mature into citizens with a greater appreciation for what being a U.S. citizen means. These citizens could return from their service with a greater capacity to be a productive part of American society. As they face their national service obligation, many individuals might do so with anxiety and reluctance, but most will later look back favorably on their completed service.

The time is here. We cannot allow things to get worse and worse until we are back in the ICU. Nothing is stopping us from going further downhill. We have *problems*, and we have to pull our heads out of the sand and make *changes*. We have to place people in power who will stop fighting each other and work together as a team to stop the wrong things from continuing and launch initiatives to do the right things.

Readers of a draft of this book came back to me with wonderful feedback on how to make it better. I made many changes. The best I saved for last. Several asked, "What are you suggesting readers do?"

- Recognize the seriousness of the problem and that more of the same is no solution.
- Apply the information in this book to your voting.
- Pass the message on to as many others as you can. The more influential they are, the better.
- Be civil in your interactions. Violence of any sort is counterproductive.

- Acknowledge that these issues are extremely difficult. There are no simple answers. It will be time consuming, and there will be undesirable side effects; however, the outcome will be better than what we have now.
- This is a democracy. Everyone has to work hard at democracy and accept the principle that the majority rules. It will not turnout well otherwise.

If we need troops on the streets of Washington for months to counter the threat of domestic terror, much more is wrong than right in American politics and governance.

I mentioned that I would make a request of you at the conclusion of the book. Here it is. If you agree that America could benefit from a comprehensive evaluation of its election system, send a letter or email to President Biden making that simple request. He frequently establishes committees to look into national issues, and this issue is certainly of national importance. If you look on the internet, you can find out how to send a letter or email to the White House. Thank you!

Endnotes

Opening Quote

1 AZQuotes, "W. Edwards Deming."

Introduction

1 Juma, "Einstein Quotes," 6.

2 Greenspan, *Age of Turbulence, 60.*

Chapter 1

1 AZQuotes, "W. Edwards Deming."

2 AZQuotes, "Youngman."

3 Jerseycam, Your Life?"

4 Wikipedia, "Passer Rating."

5 Davis, "US Election Integrity."

6 Wike, "Many Unhappy."

7 Juma, Einstein Quotes."

8 AZQuotes, "Youngman."

Chapter 2

1 Sahoo, "Problem Solving Quotes."

2 Juma, "Einstein Quotes."

3 Sahoo, "Problem Solving Quotes."

Chapter 3

1 AZQuotes, Franklin D. Roosevelt."

2 Misach, "World War II Casualties."

3 Brands, Edel, "How Woodrow Wilson Lost the Peace."

4 Wikipedia, "George Marshall."

5 EverydayPower, "Albert Einstein Quotes."

6 Wikipedia, "No Child Left Behind."

7 Glass, "US Military Draft Ends."

8 Whitelocks, "Social Security Number."

9 Macrotrends, "US Life Expectancy."

10 Anderson, "A Brief History of Medicare."

11 Poliditic, "US National Debt."

12 AZQuotes, "Henny Youngman."

13 Perry, "Maps of the Day."

14 Roos, "How Americans Have Voted."

15 Haltiwanger, "Here's Proof US Presidential Campaigns are Long."

16 Wikipedia," Donald Trump 2020 Campaign."

17 Cage, "Presidential Election Funding."

18 Wikipedia, "US Presidential Primary."

19 Neal, "Ranked-Choice-Voting."

20 AZQuotes, "W. Edwards Deming."

21 AZQuotes, "George C. Marshall."

Chapter 4

1 AZQuotes, "Dwight D. Eisenhower."

2 Apple, "Hail to the Chiefs."

3 Wikipedia, "List of Capitals."

4 AZQuotes, "George Washington."

5 Bowden, "'Idiot','Yahoo', 'Original Gorilla.'"

6 American Battlefield Trust, "Unpopular Mr. Lincoln."

7 Goodwin, *Team of Rivals.*

8 Goodreads, "Lincoln Quotes."

9 American Battlefield Trust, "Unpopular Mr. Lincoln."

10 AZQuotes, "Abraham Lincoln."

11   FDR Library & Museum, "Franklin D. Roosevelt's Presidency."

12   Kross," How Franklin Roosevelt Prepared.

13   Goodwin, *No Ordinary Times*, 57.

14   Ibid, 27.

15   AZQuotes, "Franklin D. Roosevelt."

16   Wikipedia, "Einstein-Szilard Letter."

17   Ibid

18   Norwich University Online, "Manhattan Project Scientists."

19   Wikipedia, "Leslie Groves."

20   Wikipedia, "War Production Board."

21   Wikipedia, "World War II Aircraft Production."

22   Kay's Keepers, "JFK Quote About Thomas Jefferson."

23   The University of Virginia, "About the University."

24   Polidiotic, "US National Debt."

25   McCullough, *The Path Between the Seas, 154.*

26   AZQuotes, "Theodore Roosevelt."

27   Eisenhower National History Site, "Eisenhower Military Chronology."

28   AZQuotes, "Dwight D. Eisenhower."

29   Wikipedia, "Nuclear Weapons Yield."

30   Wikipedia, "Atomic Bombing of Hiroshima and Nagasaki."

31   AZQuotes, "Harry Truman."

32   Rosenberg, "Assassination Attempt on FDR."

33   Caldera, "Fact Check."

34   Quote Ambition, "Abraham Lincoln."

35   BrainyQuotes, "Franklin D. Roosevelt."

36   AZQuotes, "Thomas Jefferson."

37   TermLimitPlege, "15 Best Term Limit Quotes."

Chapter 5

1   LIBQUOTES, "W. Edwards Deming."

2   Wikipedia, "Theory X and Theory Y."

3   McLeod, "Maslow's Hierarchy of Needs."

4   Baldrige Foundation, "Baldrige-America's Best Investment."

5   More Famous Quotes, "Malcolm Baldrige."

6   WordPress, "The Aesop Fable."

7   EverydayPower, "Einstein Quotes."

8   PeopleKeys, "William Moulton Marston."

9   Ballotpedia, "Federal Election Commission."

10   Forbes, "How GM Destroyed Its Saturn Success."

11   W. Edwards Deming Institute, "Quote on Copying Japan."

12   QuoteFancy, "Doulas McGregor."

13   Worximity, Lean Manufacturing."

14   AZQuotes, "Abraham Maslow."

Chapter 6

1   Chief Writing Wolf, "Reaction to First 2020 Debate."

2   Kiger, "St. Augustine Settlement."

3   Mutz, "Roanoke Disappeared."

4   Reference, "How Did Jamestown Survive?"

5   Wikipedia, "European Colonization of Americas."

6   Johnson, "Act of Union."

7   Wikipedia, "1790 Census."

8   Wikipedia, "George III."

9   Bunker, "Georgia Runoff Elections."

10   Celebrity Net Worth, "Ralph Warnock."

11   Niesse, "Lower GOP Turnout."

12   AZQuotes, "Franklin D. Roosevelt."

Chapter 7

1   AZQuotes, "Dwight D. Eisenhower."

2   JobMonkey, "Best Hiring Quotes."

Chapter 8

1   AZQuotes, "Norman Schwarzkopf."

2   Yahoo Search Results, "West Point Mission."

3   Association of Graduates, USMA, *Register of Graduates*,325.

4   Ibid,285.

5   Wike, Silver, and Castillo, Dissatisfaction with Performance of Democracy."

6   Bluestein, "Perdue Explores Senate Comeback."

7   Apple, "Hail to the Chiefs."

8   AZQuotes, "Norman Schwarzkopf."

9   BrainyQuotes, "Colin Powell."

10   AZQuotes, "Condoleezza Rice."

11   Inbound Marketing Summit, "Madeleine Albright Quotes."

12   BrainyQuotes, "Madeleine Albright."

13   PointerView, "Medal of Honor Recipient Speaks."

Chapter 9

1   AZQuotes, "Oliver Wendell Holmes."

2   BrainyQuotes, "Antonin Scalia."

3   AZQuotes, "Marcus Tullius Cicero."

4   Charleston, "The Brutal Beheading of Cicero."

5   AZQuotes, "Marcus Tillius Cicero."

6   AZQuotes, "Sallust."

7   BrainyQuotes, "Clarence Darrow."

8   AZQuotes, "Earl Warren."

9   AZQuotes, "Barbara Jordan."

10 AZQuotes, "W. Edwards Deming."

11 Ranker, "Funniest Lawyer Jokes."

12 Khurana, "Famous Quotes on Politics."

Chapter 10

1 BrainyQuotes, "Abraham Lincoln."

2 Wikipedia, "Battle of Gettysburg."

3 Wikipedia, "Edward Everett."

4 Mass Moments, "Edward Everett Gives Gettysburg Address."

5 Wikipedia, "Civil War Casualties."

6 Misach, "WWII Casualties."

7 Wikipedia, "Constitutional Convention."

8 NationalArchives, "The Bill of Right."

9 US Constitution-Law, "Ratification."

10 Wikipedia, "Twentieth Amendment."

11 Longley, "Federal Income Tax."

12 Wikipedia, "Sixteenth Amendment."

13 Wikipedia, "Eleventh Amendment."

14 Wolf, "25th Amendment."

15 Wikipedia, "Seventeenth Amendment."

16 Sabato, *A More Perfect Constitution*.

17 Ibid, 41.

18 Simon, *Contract to Unite America*.

19 Ibid,146.

20 Ibid, 37.

21 AZQuotes, "W. Edwards Deming."

Chapter 11

1 Sahoo, "Problem Solving Quotes."

2 Goodreads, "George Carlin Quotes."

3 Holtzman, "Deming's PDCA Cycle."

4   Editors of Encyclopaedia Britannica, "Vilfredo Pareto."

5   Goal/QPC, "The Memory Jogger."

6   Consumer Report, "Takata Airbag Recall."

7   BrainyQuotes, "Problem Solving Quoters."

Chapter 12

1   LIBQUOTES, "Theodore Roosevelt."

2   Wikipedia, "Treaty of Paris."

3   Wikipedia, "Shays' Rebellion."

4   Bartleby, "Pros and Cons of the Constitutional Convention."

5   Wike, Silver, and Castillo, "Dissatisfaction with Performance of Democracy."

6   Friedman, "American Election: How Long is too Long?"

7   Keaten and McGuirk, "What Did People in Other Countries Think?"

8   Kurtzman, "The Funniest Political Quotes."

Chapter 13

1   Goodreads, "Martin Luther Quotes."

2   Sourcesofinsight, "Seth Godin Quotes."

3   Goodreads, "Change Quotes."

4   Wikipedia, "Indiana *Pi* Bill."

5   Archives: National Commission on Service, "Mandatory Service."

6   Selective Service System, "Maintain Selective Service."

7   Glass, "US Draft Ends."

8   Turcotte, "Seven Laws of Nature."

Conclusion

1   Sahoo, "Problem Solving Quotes."

2   Seldin, "National Guard Troops."

Bibliography

American Battlefield Trust, "Evidence for the Unpopular Mr. Lincoln," accessed, 5/8/21, https://www.battlefields.org/learn/articles/evidence-unpopular-mr-lincoln.

Anderson, Steve, "A Brief History of Medicare in America," 3/24/21, https://www.medicare resources.org/basic-medicare-information/brief-history-of-medicare.

Apple, Charles, "Hail to the Chiefs," *Atlanta Journal Constitution,* 2/15/21.

Archives: National Commission on Service, "Mandatory Service Around the Globe," accessed 6/1/21, https://medium.com/@inspire2serveus/mandatory-service-around-the-globe.

Association of Graduates, USMA, *Register of Graduates and Former Cadets of the United States Military Academy, 1990 Edition,* West Point, Association of Graduates, 1990.

AZQuotes, "Top 25 Quotes by Abraham Lincoln," accessed 5/19/21 https://www.azquotes.com/author8880-Abraham_Lincoln.

AZQuotes, "Top 25 Quotes by Abraham Maslow," accessed 5/20/21, https://azquotes.com/author/9574-Abrham_Maslow.

AZQuotes, "Top 25 Quotes by Barbara Jordan," accessed 5/31/21, https://www.azquotes.com/author/7610-Barbara_Jordan.

AZQuotes, "Top 25 Quotes by Condoleezza Rice," accessed 5/20/21, https://www.azquotes.com/author/12281-Condoleezza -Rice.

AZQuotes, "Top 25 Quotes by Dwight D. Eisenhower," accessed 5/8/21, https://www.azquotes.com/author/4403_Dwight_D_Eisenhower.

AZQuotes, "Top 25 Quotes by Earl Warren," accessed 5/31/21, https://azquotescom/author/15307-Earl_Warren.

AZQuotes, "Top 25 Quotes by Franklin D. Roosevelt," accessed 5/5/21, https://www.azquotes.com/author/2604Franklin_D_Roosevelt.

AZQuotes, "Top 25 Quotes by George C. Marshall," accessed 5/21/21, https://www.azquotes.com/author/9510_George_C_Marshall.

AZQuotes, "Top 25 Quotes by George Washington," accessed 5/8/21, https://www.azquotes.com/author/15324_George_Washington.

AZQuotes, "Top 25 Quotes by Harry S. Truman," accessed 5/30/21, https://www.azquotes.com/author/14187_Harry_S_Truman.

AZQuotes, "Top 25 Quotes by Henny Youngman Quotes," accessed 1/25/21, https://www.azquotes.com/author/16107-Henny-Youngman.

AZQuotes, "Top 25 Quotes by Marcus Tillius Cicero," accessed 2/19/21, https://www.azquotes.com/author/2894 - Marcus_Tullius_Cicero.

AZQuotes, "TOP 25 Quotes by Norman Schwarzkopf," accessed 5/20/21, https://www.azquotes.com/author/13189-Norman_Schwarzkopf.

AZQuotes, "Top 25 Quotes by Oliver Wendell Holmes, Jr.," accessed 5/30/21, https://www.azquotes.com/author/6846-Oliver_Wendell_Holmes_Jr.

AZQuotes, "Top 25 Quotes by Sallust," accessed 5/31/21, https://azquotes.com/author/3794-Sallust.

AZQuotes, "Top 25 Quotes by Theodore Roosevelt," accessed 5/30/21, https://www.azquotes.com/author/12606-Theodore_Roosevelt.

AZQuotes, "Top 25 Quotes by Thomas Jefferson," accessed 6/4/21, https://azquotes.com/author/17392-Thomas_Jefferson.

AZQuotes, "Top 25 Quotes by W. Edwards Deming," accessed 4/24/21, https://www.azquotes.com/author/3858-W-Edwards-Deming.

Baldrige Foundation, "Baldrige-America's Best Investment," accessed 5/21/21, https://www.baldrigefoundation.org/who-we-are/history.html.

Ballotpedia, "Federal Election Commission," accessed 5/20/21, https://ballotpedia.org/Federal_Election_Commission.

Bartleby, "The Pros and Cons of the Constitutional Convention of 1787", accessed 2/24/21, https://www.bartleby.com/essay/The-Pros-and-Cons-of-the -Constitutional-PCFCUMN9R6.

Bluestein, Greg, "Perdue Explores Senate Comeback," *Atlanta Journal Constitution,*2/17/21.

Bowden, Mark, "'Idiot', 'Yahoo,' 'Original Gorilla': How Lincoln was Dissed in His Day," *Atlantic,* 6/2013, https://the Atlantic.com/magazine/archive/2013/06/Abraham-lincoln-is-an-idiot/309304/.

BrainyQuotes, "Abraham Lincoln Quotes," accessed 6/5/21, https://www.brainyquotes.com/authors/abraham-lincoln-quotes.

BrainyQuotes, "Antonio Scalia Quotes," accessed 5/31/21, https://www.brainyquotes.com/author/antonio-scalia-quotes.

BrainyQuotes, "Clarence Darrow Quotes," accessed 5/30/21, https://www.brainyquotes.com/author/clarence-darrow-quotes.

BrainyQuotes, "Colin Powell Quotes," accessed 5/20/21, https://www.brainyquotes.com/authors/colin-powell-quotes.

BrainyQuotes, "Franklin D. Roosevelt Quotes," accessed, 5/30/21 https://brainyquotes.com/quotes/franklin_d_roosevelt_40295.

BrainyQuotes, "Madeleine Albright Quotes," accessed,5/20/21, https://www.brainyquotes.com/author/madeleine-albright-quotes.

BrainyQuotes, "Problem Solving Quotes," accessed 5/31/21, https://www.braineyquotes.com/topics/problem-solving-quotes.

Brands, Hal and Edel, Charles, "How Woodrow Wilson Lost the Peace," 1/30/19, https://the americaninterest.com/2019/01/30/how-woodrow-wilson-lost-the-peace/.

Bunker, Theodore, "Georgia Runoff Elections Break Spending Records," 1/5/21, https://www.newsmax.com/newsfront/georgia-runoff-election-record/2021/05/id/1004379/.

Cage, Julia, "How Barack Obama Spurred the End of America's Public Presidential Funding System," 4/27/2020, https://promarket.org/2021/04/27/how-barack-obama-spurred-the-end-of-the-public-presidential -funding-system.

Caldera, Camille, "Fact Check: Claimed Abraham Lincoln Quote About 'Internal Rottenness' is Fake," 1/3/21, https://www.usatoday.com/story/news/factcheck/2021/03/fact -check-abraham-lincoln-quote-internal-rottenness-fake/410769001/. (Abraham Lincoln and John Lloyd James expressed the same thought using different words.)

Celebrity Net Worth, "Raphael Warnock Net Worth," accessed 5/21/21, https://www.celebritynetworth.com/richest-politicians/democrats/raphael-net-worth/.

Chief Writing Wolf, "How the World Reacted to the First 2020 U. S. Presidential Candidate Debate," 10/3/20, https: chiefwritingwolf.com.tag/jussi-hanhimaki/.

Charleston, L. J., "The Brutal Beheading of Cicero," 12/9/16, https://www.the morning bulletin.com.an/news/the-brutal-beheading-of-cicero-romes-greatest-pol./3596904/.

Consumer Report, "Takata Airbag Recall: Everything You Need to Know," 4/21/21, https://www.consumer report.org/car-recalls-defects/takata-airbag-recall-everything-you-need-to-know/.

Davis, Elliott, "U.S. Election Integrity Compares Poorly to Other Democracies," 10/7/20, https://www.usnews,com/news/best countries/articles/2020-10-07/us-elections-compare-poorly-to-other-democracies-research-shows.

Editors of Encyclopedia Britannica, "Vilfredo Pareto," accessed 3/6/21, https://www.britannica.com/biography/vilfredo-pareto.

Eisenhower National History Site, "Eisenhower Military Chronology," accessed 2/4/21, https://www.nsp.gov/features,eise/jrranger/chronomil1htm.

Everydaypower, "60 About Einstein Quotes About Love, Imagination and war," accessed 5/29/21, https://everydaypower.com/albert-einstein-quotes.

FDR Library & Museum, "Franklin D. Roosevelts Presidency" accessed 5/21/21, https://www.archives.gov/.

Forbes, "How GM Destroyed Its Saturn Success," accessed 5/20/21, https://www.forbes.com/2010/03/08/saturn-gm-innovation-leadership-managing- failure.html.

Friedman, Uri, "American Elections. How long Is too Long?" 10/5/16, https://www.theatlantic.com/international/archives/2016/10/us-elections/longest-world/5015801.

Glass, Andrew, "U. S. Military Draft Ends, Jan. 27, 1973," 1/27/2012,https://www.politico.com,/story/2012/01/us-military-draft-ends-jan-27-1973-0720.

Goal/QPC, "The Memory Jogger: A Pocket Guide for Continuous Improvement," 2nd Edition, Methuen, Ma: Goal/QPC, 1988.

Goodreads, "Abraham Lincoln> Quotes>Quotable Quotes," accessed 5/9/21, https://goodreads.com/quotes/67212-well-i-wish-some-of-you-would-tell-me-the.

Goodreads, "Change Quotes," accessed 4/30/21, https://www.goodreads.com/quotes/tag/change.

Goodreads, "George Carlin Quotes," accessed 4/30/21, https://www.goodreads.com/quotes 39152-i-put-a-dollar-in-a-change-machine-nothing-changed.

Goodreads, "Martin Luther Quotes," accessed 4/30/21, https://www.goodreads.com/author/quotes/29874, Martin Luther.

Goodwin, Doris Kearns, *Team of Rivals: The Political Genius of Abraham Lincoln*, New York, Simon & Schuster, 2005.

Goodwin, Doris Kerns, *No Ordinary Times*, New York, Simon & Schuster, 1994.

Greenspan, Alan, *The Age of Turbulence: Adventures in a New World*, New York, The Penguin Press, 2007.

Haltiwanger, John, "Here's Proof US President Campaigns Are Way Too F-cking Long," 3/29/16, https://www.elitedaily.com/news/politics/presidential-campaigns-way-too-long/1436932.

Holtzman, Mark, "W. Edwards Deming's PDCA Cycle for Continuous Improvement," accessed 3/6/21, https://www.dummies.com/business/operations-management/w-edwards-demings-pdca-cycle-for-continuous-improvement.

Inbound Marketing Summit, "Madeleine Albright Quotes," accessed 5/20/21, https://inboundmarketingsummit.com/madeleine-albright-quotes/.

Jerseycam, "How's Your Life/Wife? Compared to What?" accessed 5/1/21, https://jerseycam.com/index.php/2020/11/18/hows-your-wife-compared-to-what.

JobMonkey, "18 of the Best Hiring Quotes and Sayings," accessed 5/24/21, https://www.jobmonkey.com/employer-insights-hiring-quotes-sayings/.

Johnson, Ben, "The Act of Union," accessed 5/20/21, https://www.historic-uk.com/HistoryUK/Historyof Britain/The-Act-of-Union/.

Juma, Norbert, "60 Albert Einstein Quotes About Love, Imagination, and War," 9/23/20, https:/everydaypower.com/albert-einstein-quotes/.

Kay's Keepers, "JFK Quote About Thomas Jefferson," 7/25/11, https://KaysKeepers.blogspot.com/2011/07/jfk-quote-about-thomas-jefferson.html.

Keaton, Jamie and McGuirk, Rod, "What Did People in Other Countries Think of that Presidential Debate? It's Not Great," 9/30/20, https://www.chicagotribune.com/election-2020/ct-presidential-debate-other-countries-20200930.

Khurana, Simran, "Famous Quotes That Reveal the True Face of Politics," accessed 5/22/21, https://www.liveabout.com/famous-quotes-about-politicians-2832308.

Kiger, Patrick, "How St. Augustine Became the First European Settlement in America," 9/29/20, https://www.history.com/news/st.-augustine-first-american-settlement.

Kross, Peter, "How Franklin D. Roosevelt Prepared the U. S. for World War II," accessed 4/30/21, https://warfarehistoorynetwork.com/2017/01/04/how-franklin-d-roosevelt-prepared-us-for-wwii/.

Kurtzman, Daniel, "The Funniest Political Quotes of All Times," 1/6/19, https://www.liveabout.com/funniest-political-quotes-of-all-times-4078944.

LIBQUOTES, "Theodore Roosevelt Quotes About Government," accessed 5/31/21, https://libquotes.com/theodore-roosevelt/quotes/government.

LIBQUOTES, "W. Edwards Deming Quotes," accessed 5/19/21, https://libquotes.com/w-edwards-deming/2.

Longley, Robert, "History of the U. S. Federal Income Tax," 11/3/19,https://www.houghcom/history-of-the-us-federal-income-tax-332160.

Macrotrends, "U. S. Life Expectancy 1950-2021," accessed 5/21/21, https://www.macrotrends.net/countries/USA/united-states-life-expectancy.

Mass Moments, "November 19, 1863 Edward Everett Gives Gettysburg Address," accessed 6/5/21, https://massmoments.org/moment-details/Edward-everett-gives-gettysburg-address.html.

McCullough, David, *The Path Between the Seas: The Creation of the Panama Canal*, New York, Simon & Schuster, 1977.

McLeod, Saul, "Maslow's Hierarchy of Needs," 12/29/20, https://www.simplypsychology.org/maslow,html.

Misach, John, "WW II Casualties by Country, 8/15/19, https://www.worldatlas.com/articles/wwii-casualties-by-country.html.

More Famous Quotes, "Malcolm Baldrige Quotes," accessed 5/20/21, https://www.morefamousquotes.com/topics/malcolm-baldrige-quotes/.

Mutz, Phil, "In 1587, 115 People Disappeared from Roanoke After Carving One Word into A Tree," 10/19/15, https://littlethings.com/lifestyle/lost-colony-of-roanoke.

National Archives, "The Bill of Rights: How Did It Happen?" accessed 6/5/21, https://www.archives.gov/founding-docs/bill-of-rights/how-did-it-happen.

Neal, Jeff, "Ranked-Choice Voting Explained," 10/26/20, https://today.law.harvard.edu/ranked-choice-voting-explained/.

Niesse, Mark and Peebles, Jennifer, "Lower GOP Turnout Helped Flip Senate, " *Atlanta Journal Constitution*, 2/11/21.

Norwich University Online, "Who Were the Manhattan Project Scientists," 8/1/17, https://online.norwich.edu/academicprograms/resources/who-were-the-manhattan-project-scientists.

Perry, Mark, "Maps of the Day: Travel Times from NYC in 1800, 1830, 1857 and 1930," 10/5/16, https://www.aei.org/carpe-diem/maps-of-the-day-travel-times-from-nyc-in-1800-1830-1857-and-1900.

PeopleKeys, "William Moulton Marston, Founder of DISC," accessed 5/20/21, https://peoplekeys.com/about-disc/william-moulton-marston.

PointerView, "Medal of Honor Recipient Speaks to Plebes on Leadership," accessed 5/20/21 https://www.pointerview,com/2016/07/14/medal-of-honor-recipient-speaks-to-plebes-on-leadership/.

Polidiotic, "U. S. National Debt by Year," accessed 5/5/21, https://www.polidiotic.com/by-the-numbers-/us-national-debt-by-year/.

Quote Ambition, "70 Abraham Lincoln Quotes," accessed 1/25/21, https://www.quoteambition.com/abraham-lincoln-quotes/.

Quote Fancy, "Top 10 Douglas McGregor Quotes," accessed 5/20/21, https://quotefancy.com/douglas-mcgregor-quoted.

Ranker, "Funniest Lawyer Jokes/ Funny Joke List for Lawyers," accessed 2/19/21, https://www.ranker.com/list/lawyer-jokes/jack-napier.

Reference, "How Did Jamestown Survive?" 3/5/20, https://www.reference.com/history/did-jamestown-survive.

Roos, Dave, "How Americans Have Voted Through History: From Voices to Screens," accessed 5/6/21, https://www.history.com/news/voting-elections-ballots-electronic.

Rosenberg, Jennifer, "Assassination Attempt on FDR," 3/1/19, https://www.thoughtco.com/assassination-attemt-on-fdr-1779297.

Sabato, Larry, *A More Perfect Constitution: 23 Proposals to Revitalize Our Constitution and Make America a Fairer Country*, New York, Walker Publishing Company, Inc., 2007.

Sahoo, Manoranjan, "Problem Solving Quotes: Solve Your Problem in Your Own Way," 7/12/20, https://Knoasw.com/problem-solving-quotes/.

Seldin, Jeff, "Pentagon Says 2300 National Guard Troops to Stay at Capitol Through May 23 as a Post-Riot Review Calls for Increased Security," USA News, 3/10/21, https://www.rt.com/usa/517670-national -guard--capitol-staying/.

Selective Service System, "National Commission Multi-Year Study Affirms the Nation Needs to Maintain the Selective Service," accessed 3/10/21, https://www.sss.gov/news/national-commission-final report/.

Simon, Neal, *Contract to Unite America: Ten Reforms to Reclaim Our Republic*, Canada, Real Clear Publishing,2020.

Sourcesofinsight, "The Best Seth Godin Quotes that Will Make You Think," accessed 4/30/21, https://sourcesofinsight.com/seth-goodin-quotes/.

Term Limits Pledge, "15 Best Term Limit Quotes," 8/1/19, https://termlimitspledge.org/post/15-best-term-limit-quotes.

The University o0f Virginia, "About the University," accessed 5/30/21, https://www.virginia.edu/aboutuva.

Turcotte, Paul, "The Seven Laws of Nature," 12/4/11, https://insidedestiny.com/the-seven-laws-of-nature.

U. S. Constitution-LAWS, "Ratification of the Constitution," 10/23/20, https://constitution/laws-com/ratification-of-the-constitution.

W. Edwards Deming Institute, "American Management Thinks that It Can Just Copy from Japan but They Don't Know What to Copy," accessed 3/20/21, https:deming.org/quotes/10176/.

Whitelocks, Sadie, "Social Security Number? 00-0000-001. Woman Who Was First to Receive Welfare Check Remembered 75 Years After the System Was Born," 7/30/15, https://www.dailymail.co.uk/news/article-2932568/Meet-Ida-May-Fuller-recipient-1st-social-security-check.html.

Wike, Richard; Silver, Laura; and Castillo, Alexandra, "Dissatisfaction with Performance of Democracy is Common in Many Nations," 4/29/19, https://www.pewresearch.org/global/2019/04/29/dissatisfaction-with-performance-0f-democracy-is-common-in-many-nations.

Wike, Richard; Simmons, Katie; Stokes, Bruce; et. al, "Many Unhappy with Current Political System," 10/16/17, https://www.pewrearch.org/global/2017/10/16/many-unhappy-with-current-political-system/.

Wikipedia, "1790 United States Census," accessed 6/5/21, https://en.wikipedia.org/wiki/1790_United_States_census.

Wikipedia, "American Civil War Casualties," accessed 6/5/21, https://en.wikipedia.org/wiki/American_Civil_War_Casualties.

Wikipedia, "Atomic Bombing of Hiroshima and Nagasaki," accessed 5/26/21, https://en.wikipedia.org/wiki/atomic_bombing_of_Hiroshima_and_Nagasaki.

Wikipedia, "Battle of Gettysburg," accessed 6/5/21,
    https://en.wikipedia.org/wiki/Battle_of_Gettysburg.

Wikipedia, "Constitutional Convention (United States),"
    accessed 6/5/21,
    https://en.wikipedia.org/wiki/Constitutional_Convention_(U
    nited_States).

Wikipedia, "Donald Trump 2020 Presidential Campaign,"
    accessed 5/29/21, https://en.wikipedia.org/wiki/Donald-
    Trump_2020_presidential-campaign.

Wikipedia, "Edward Everett," accessed 6/5/21,
    https://en.wikipedia.org/wiki/Edward_Everett.

Wikipedia, "Einstein-Szilard Letter," accessed 5/30/21,
    https://en.wikipedia.org/wiki/Einstein-Szilard_letter.

Wikipedia, "Eleventh Amendment to the United States
    Constitution," accessed 6/5/21,
    https://en.wikipedia.org/wiki/Eleventh_Amendment_to-the-
    United_States_Constitution.

Wikipedia, "George C. Marshall," accessed 5/5/21,
    https://en.wikipedia.org/wiki/George-c.-marshall.

Wikipedia, "George III," accessed 5/20/21,
    https://en.wikipedia.org/wiki/George_III.

Wikipedia, "Indiana Pi Bill," accessed 5/28/21,
    https://en.wikipedia.org/wiki/Indiana_Pi_Bill.

Wikipedia, "Leslie Groves," accessed 5/30/21,
    https://en.wikipedia.org/wiki/Leslie_Groves.

Wikipedia, "List of Capitals in the United States," accessed
    5/12/21, https://en.wikipedia.org/wiki/List_of_capitals_in-the-
    United-States.

Wikipedia, "No Child Left Behind Act," accessed 5/5/21,
    https://en.wikipedia.org/wiki/No-Child-Left-Behind-Act.

Wikipedia, "Nuclear Weapons Yield," accessed 5/26/21
https://en.wikipedia.org/wiki/Nuclear_weapons_yield.

Wikipedia, "Passer Rating," accessed 4/24/21,
https://en.wikipedia.org/wiki/Passer-rating.

Wikipedia, "Seventeenth Amendment to the United States
Constitution," accessed 6/5/21,
https://en.wikipedia.org/wiki/seventeenth-amendment-to-
the-united-states-constitution.

Wikipedia, "Shays' Rebellion," accessed 2/24/21
https://en.wikipedia.org/wiki/Shays%27_Rebellion.

Wikipedia, "Sixteenth Amendment to the United States
Constitution," accessed 6/5/21,
https://en.wikipedia.org/wiki/Sixteenth_Amendment_to-the-
United_States_Constitution.

Wikipedia, "Theory X and Theory Y," accessed 2/8/21,
https://en.wikipedia.org/wiki/Theory-X-and-Theory-Y."

Wikipedia, "Treaty of Paris (1783)" accessed 5/31/21
https://en.wikipedia.org/wiki/Treaty_of_Paris.

Wikipedia, "Twentieth Amendment to the United States
Constitution," accessed 6/5/21,
https://en.wikipedia.org/wiki/Twentieth_Amendment_to-the-
United_States_Constitution.

Wikipedia, "United States Presidential Primary," accessed
5/19/21,
https://en.wikipedia.org/wiki/United_States_Presidential
_Primary.

Wikipedia, "War Production Board, " accessed 5/30/21,
https://en.wikipedia.org/wiki/War_Production_Board.

Wikipedia, "World War II Aircraft Production," accessed 5/8/21
https://en.wikipedia.org/wiki/World_War_II_aircraft_production.

Wolf, Zachary, "What's the 25th Amendment and How Does it
    Work?" 1/11/21,https://www.cnn.com/2021/01/06/politics,25th-
    amendment-explainer/index.html.

Word Press, "The Aesop Fable-The Scorpion and The Frog,"
    accessed 2/9/21, https://thescorpionandthefrog.com/about/.

Worximity, "Introduction to Lean Manufacturing Principles,"
    accessed 6/2/21, https://www.worximity.com/en/introduction-
    to-lean-manufacturing-principles.

Yahoo Search Results, "West Point Mission Statement," accessed
    2/16/21, https://search.yahoo.com/search?p=West+.